Sloterdijk

Key Contemporary Thinkers

Sloterdijk

Jean-Pierre Couture

polity

First published in 2016 by Polity Press

Polity Press
65 Bridge Street
Cambridge CB2 1UR, UK

Polity Press
350 Main Street
Malden, MA 02148, USA

ISBN-13: 978-0-7456-6380-7
ISBN-13: 978-0-7456-6381-4 (pb)

A catalogue record for this book is available from the British Library.

Library of Congress Cataloging-in-Publication Data

Couture, Jean-Pierre, 1975–
   Sloterdijk / Jean-Pierre Couture.
      pages cm. – (Key contemporary thinkers)
   Includes bibliographical references and index.
      ISBN 978-0-7456-6380-7 (hardcover : alk. paper) – ISBN 0-7456-6380-X
(hardcover : alk. paper) – ISBN 978-0-7456-6381-4 (pbk. : alk. paper) –
ISBN 0-7456-6381-8 (pbk. : alk. paper)   1. Sloterdijk, Peter,
1947–   I. Title.
   B3332.S254C68 2015
   193–dc23
         2015012743

Typeset in 10 on 11.5 pt Palatino
by Toppan Best-set Premedia Limited
Printed and bound in the UK by Clays Ltd, St Ives plc.

For further information on Polity, visit our website:
politybooks.com

For Roman, sun of December

Contents

Acknowledgments

I could not have written this book without the support of a special circle of friends, colleagues, and students. First, I would like to thank Emma Hutchinson and David Winters of Polity for positive initial contact with regard to the book proposal, and Pascal Porcheron, also of Polity, for his patience, trust, and work on the production of the manuscript.

The earliest version of this book was tentatively discussed in a seminar held at La Casa Obscura in Montréal. Philippe-David Blanchette, Marc-Olivier Castagner, Hubert Gendron-Blais, Robert Hébert, Simon Hogue, Simon Labrecque, and Sylvain Munger offered, on those occasions, brilliant comments that helped me rethink it.

I would like to express my gratitude to my translator, Richard Ashby, who was also part of that seminar and whose expertise, diligence, and patience added considerably to my confidence about the project. A very special thanks goes to my Masters students Alex Del Duca and Jonah Clifford, who carefully read and commented on the advanced version; the final product is the better for it.

I must also acknowledge the beneficial influence of my old friend and supervisor Jean-Marc Piotte, without whose example and encouragement I would not have considered becoming a professor. It was under his tutelage that I developed a better work ethic and a sense of political and intellectual commitment.

Many students, too, have provided me with kind words over the last few years, and I would like to thank them: Frédérique Bélanger, Laurence Bernier-Renaud, Caroline Brouillette, Ducakis Désinat, Xavier Dionne, Nicholas DuBois, Mélanie Dufour, Anaïs Elboujdaïni, Jean-Philip Guy, Isabelle Hêtu, David B. Hyppia, Susan Kim, Jonathan Lalande-Bernatchez, †Rémi Latulippe, Dylan Peaks, Guillaume Poirier, Lana Racković, and Maxime Wawanoloath. Appreciation also goes to the office staff of my department, Gail Petrin and Sylvie Lachapelle, who bring much life and spirit to our milieu.

I must not forget to mention Sophie Bernard-Piché, Mathieu Bois-lard, Nathalie Burlone, Anne-Marie D'Aoust, Gabrielle Gauvin, David Grondin, Yves Lavoie, Marie Leahey, Jean-Charles Saint-Louis, and Patrick Sénécal. I warmly thank you all for your humor, lust for life, and precious friendship.

I recognize that this research would not have been possible without the financial assistance of the Social Sciences and Humanities Research Council of Canada. It would have been simply impossible without colleagues such as Christian Rouillard and Micheline Lessard, who fought for my academic freedom at the University of Ottawa in recent years. I would like to express my deepest gratitude to them.

Finally, my warmest thanks go to my wife, Stéphanie, without whose love and support this book would never have been started. My greatest debt is to her.

Abbreviations

Introduction

Interpreting an author's work during his or her lifetime is not without its many challenges. One does not have the luxury of either a definitive corpus or the passive silence of authors who are no longer with us. This said, an exhaustive introduction to Peter Sloterdijk is a needed and legitimate undertaking. Since the first decade of the 2000s, his newly translated works have piqued the interest of an English-speaking public that had not really followed his thought beyond the 1980s. Jochen Schulte-Sasse (1940–2012) introduced Sloterdijk to the English-speaking world when, in the series he edited at the University of Minnesota Press, *Critique of Cynical Reason* was published in 1987, quickly followed by *Thinker on Stage* in 1989. Following a gap of two decades in the reception and translation of Sloterdijk's work, three English-language publishers – Polity, Semiotext(e), and Columbia University Press – have all had a hand in the recent effort. This critical work took shape around publications edited by Stuart Elden: the special issue (co-edited with Eduardo Mendieta and Nigel Thrif) of *Society and Space* in 2009 and the *Sloterdijk Now* collection in 2012. Along with these substantive contributions, the Dutch philosopher Sjoerd van Tuinen was one of the first to critically study Sloterdijk's work, and the German author Hans-Jürgen Heinrichs published a general introduction to Sloterdijk's thought in 2011.[1] The present book seeks to relate the rise of this distinguished contemporary philosopher and notorious public intellectual by drawing out the vivacity of both his recent and older published work. In doing so, it hopes to enable a wider reading public to navigate his fertile and at times provocative intellectual output.

This exercise is critical in nature. As such, I often overlook Sloterdijk's self-descriptions or his occasional shots across the bows of the influential commentators or translators of his work whose judgment or mere stupidity he fears:

One of the distinctive signs of the thought of our times is to have questioned the concept of the author. Among other things, this thought is in the process of suppressing the theological ballast that had been used to support the idea of the old Europe, that is, the human paternity of intellectual production. Since then, contemporary authors, perhaps more so than their historical predecessors, have had reasons and opportunities to examine the abysmal difference between their personal intentions and how their work is received.[2]

By their very nature, the secrets of intentions are impossible to plumb. I therefore concentrate on texts, their arguments and their contributions, the debates to which they gave rise and the softening of some of the biting arguments after their initial formulation. Though the behind-the-scenes publication intrigues and battles to the death in Germany's intellectual landscape are discussed in chapter 4, it should be noted that they color several remarks throughout the book. The reason is that Sloterdijk constantly redraws the boundaries between provocation and theory by sitting astride a hybrid beast composed of art and philosophy, which he refers to as centauric literature. Lastly, my political science background often leads me to assess Sloterdijk's arguments in political and ideological terms as they unfold in debates in which he has willingly participated. If there is a constant in these few political discords, it touches upon the intrinsic limits of Sloterdijk's project; that is, the fact that he so strongly describes his work as emerging from Nietzsche can only put it on a collision course with the foundations of democracy. Like his forerunner, Sloterdijk neither is nor wants to be a theorist of equality. Far from rejecting the fecundity of this provocative, dissensual body of work, this remark seeks only to disclose my own reservations and my own fears. More serenely, I do not think that the collective reception of Sloterdijk's thought will prevent him from perhaps attaining the ranks of those essential thinkers whose works are forever discussed. Indeed, "classic texts are those that survive their interpretations" (TS 3).

Born in 1947 in Karlsruhe, Germany, Sloterdijk studied philosophy and German literature in Munich and Hamburg before shifting his interest to structuralism and the thought of Michel Foucault. In 1976, he completed his doctoral research on autobiographical material produced in Weimar Germany. Afterwards, he disappeared momentarily from the intellectual scene and permanently from the world of academic philosophy.

Around 1980, Sloterdijk spent some time in Poona, India, at an ashram that was home to Bhagwan Shree Rajneesh's sect. Born as Rajneesh Chandra Mohanin in 1931, "Bhagwan" (the "divine") previously taught philosophy and psychology at the University of Jalapur.

At his Poona ashram, he directed an institute for comparative research on religions that attracted tens of thousands of Westerners between 1974 and 1981. Following his move to Oregon in the United States, "Bhagwan," who had changed his name to "Osho," showed his darker side when he became the guru of an oppressive sect. On the heels of problems with the FBI, he returned to Poona, where he died in 1990. Sloterdijk regularly returns to both his Poona experiences and Bhagwan, whom he ranked among the twentieth century's four greatest proponents of Indian spirituality (MCL 280). As a testament, no doubt, to Bhagwan's formative influence on the younger Sloterdijk, the lessons learned in Poona are never far removed from the theoretical stances adopted in his later thought: release of the body, anti-kinetic slowness, post-rational breathing, pre-individualist fusion, and athletic exercise in vertical tension.

The two volumes of *Kritik der zynischen Vernunft* (*Critique of Cynical Reason*) were published in 1983. With this inaugural work, Sloterdijk immediately imposed himself as the author of a cult book that sold more than 120,000 copies in Germany before being translated into English in 1987. It remains post-war German philosophy's greatest success. A new philosopher had been born, who then began to craft a cycle of psychopolitical works focused on the spirit of his times.

Associated with the 1968 intellectual generation, referred to as "APO" (*Außerparlamentarische Opposition*; i.e., Extra-Parliamentary Opposition), Sloterdijk participated in neither the Marxist nor the anarchist or left-wing terrorist fringe, but rather in the hedonist fringe. This counter-cultural trait would subsequently lead him to comb through the legacy of Romanticism for the conditions of a Dionysian materialism arising out of the necessary rejection of critical theory.

Indeed, Sloterdijk came to want to sever all ties with the Frankfurt School as he intensified his efforts to find resources in the works of Nietzsche and Heidegger for a genuinely frontal critique of modernity. This project would have been impossible without the efforts of a few forerunners who had been working since the early 1960s on remodeling the thought of Nietzsche and Heidegger within the framework of the consumer society. These forerunners are from France and took their inspiration from Henri Lefebvre and Jean Beaufret. Going against all orthodox thought, Lefebvre attempted to create a dialogue between Marx and Nietzsche in addition to contributing to the birth of a philosophy of space. For his part, Beaufret paved the way for introducing Heidegger's thought in France. His efforts were soon exploited and amplified by a subsequent generation personified by Jacques Derrida and Jean-Luc Nancy.

France is Sloterdijk's adopted intellectual homeland.[3] Like Heine in the mid-nineteenth century, he has worked at making German thought known in France and French thought known in Germany. The flow of this trade route across the Rhine is perhaps tilted in the latter direction because he ardently wants to make up for Germany's lag in appreciating the contributions of Nietzsche and Heidegger to contemporary thought about emancipation. The libertarian-slanted reappropriation of the Nietzschean and Heideggerian canons has been the accepted reading by French poststructuralists such as Foucault, Deleuze, and Derrida, and it is for this reason that Sloterdijk's adoption of this posture rightly saw him labeled as the "most French-leaning of German philosophers."[4]

Indeed, Sloterdijk's relationship with France is both friendly and close. He spends a good part of each year in France and maintains a place in a network of influential thinkers. He periodically collaborates with notable conservative thinkers such as Alain Finkielkraut[5] and Régis Debray,[6] and has developed a long-lasting friendship with Bruno Latour, who has contributed significantly to making Sloterdijk's work known in France.[7] Although Sloterdijk did not have the opportunity to meet Foucault before the latter's early demise in 2004, he assigns him an important place in his work and takes inspiration from his last classes at the Collège de France in his thoughts about ethics (MCL 148–59). Lastly, Sloterdijk mourned the death of Derrida in 1984 by immediately paying homage to the Derridian specter, which he links with figures from the past and present-day friendships.[8]

This closeness, however, is not without a few disagreements and disappointments. In 2005, for example, Sloterdijk bitterly reproached the French left for refusing to accept the European constitution project even though Germany had supported it. This disagreement also led him to say that the Franco-German partnership had faded somewhat in the general indifference to the commemoration of the fortieth anniversary of the Franco-German treaty of friendship, signed by Konrad Adenauer and Charles de Gaulle in 1963. Although he was named Commandeur de l'Ordre des Arts et des Lettres of the French Republic in 2006, Sloterdijk quickly began to lament this shared indifference, which he claimed could be viewed as a consolation prize given to long-lasting peace. At the very least, his tender sarcasm recommends the virtues of shared indifference to all countries at war:

> Do it the same way that we did, don't be too interested in each other! And be careful how you choose your foreign correspondents for the newspapers, make sure that those reporting from neighbouring countries are sure to bore their readers to death! Only in this way can those happily separated from one another live in friendship and peace with each other. (TPWP 49)

Although he is more often than not disappointed with the politics of his times, which he views as lacking vision and ambition, it needs to be noted that Sloterdijk's intellectual trajectory is lacking in neither. He was appointed as rector in 2001 of the Karlsruhe University of Arts and Design, a setting that provides him with a research laboratory in which contemporary thought, aesthetic theory, and visual arts work side by side. Under the supervision of his friends and collaborators Boris Groys and Peter Weibel, the university regularly organizes important exhibitions that explore the fertile nature of the meeting of these fields.[9] The iconoclastic nature of this school has certainly provided Sloterdijk's philosophical undertaking with a creative physical and mental space and a freedom of inquiry unbounded by the imperatives of university specialization. Indeed, Sloterdijk explores the possibilities of writing that brings together form and content, literature and philosophy, and art and thought within the framework of an undertaking that operates as much in terms of expressiveness as of permissiveness. To be sure, he has taken advantage of his considerable institutional independence to construct a research climate free from academic auto-censorship. Moreover, he openly mistrusts the milieu of professional philosophy, which, he says, now settles for "avoiding mistakes" and "minimizing declarations":

> Today philosophy is at its most professional when it may explain how it would say something, in the extraordinary case that it would say something. However, it is far too reflexive to say anything; it is afraid of relevant worldviews like a child fears the fire s/he touched once. Instead, from the earlier love of wisdom a multinational concern specialized in error avoidance has emerged, which promises security as a first principle. Modern philosophy achieves its highest goal in speaking most minimally and in its refrainment from too far-fetched statements.[10]

This extra-academic position certainly enables him to enjoy the largesse of an exploratory and speculative approach that is not accountable to the surveillance of an unlettered dean.

This considerable autonomy recalls Albert William Levi's description of the era of gentlemen in early modern times. Before the age of professionals of academic philosophy, these gentlemen generated and invested their cultural capital outside of universities sponsored then by theology and now by impact factor management.[11] Sloterdijk's reputation is made up from various forms of capital and redefines the framework of intellectual engagement. From 2002 to 2012, he co-hosted, along with his good friend Rüdiger Safranski, *Das philosophische Quartett*, a monthly television program broadcast on the German ZDF network. As a public intellectual, he never refuses interview requests from major German media outlets on matters relating to current affairs. Moreover, he is regularly solicited by high-level authorities to advise public servants. Lastly, his books are not only bestsellers, but also feats of erudition and literary quality that have earned him prestigious awards: the Ernst Robert Curtius Prize for Essay Writing (1993), the Christian Kellerer Prize for the future of philosophical thought (2001), the Austrian Decoration for Science and Art (2005), and the Sigmund Freud Prize for Scientific Prose (2005), awarded in the past to Hannah Arendt, Hans Georg Gadamer, and Jürgen Habermas.

Sloterdijk views his work as a medicine of civilization, willing intoxication and theory of immersion. His essays are both literary and philosophical; they come at times from the angle of very concise, philosophy-based commentaries on a political conjuncture, and at other times reveal themselves as much more ambitious, nearly-1,000-page opuses. For Sloterdijk, philosophy is about storytelling and forms: the author's capacity for expression at several levels simultaneously (philosophical erudition and working within the framework of canons, mixed with the irony and humor of a metaphorical language accessible to an educated public and non-professional philosophers) and the regular use of iconography (many images projected over and alongside a discourse and which themselves present an argument) all bear witness to his singularity. Yet there is nothing certain about merging entertainment and knowledge. Sloterdijk is indeed entertaining, but does he philosophize? For many observers, therein lies the question.

This book has five main chapters, each of which covers one of the five approaches used in Sloterdijk's work. Chapter 1 draws out the initial motives underlying his work devoted to the study of cultural crises or psychopolitics. Chapters 2 and 3 focus on the anthropological and spatial narratives that support the Great Narrative of the human adventure. This story of anthropotechnics and spherology is strongly impregnated with Heideggerian thought, which Sloterdijk explores in an unprecedented manner. This positioning within the thought of Freiburg and the grandiloquence of Nietzsche would inevitably lead Sloterdijk to a confrontation with the Frankfurt School. In chapter 4, the quarrels with Jürgen Habermas and Axel Honneth shed light on Sloterdijk's ideological coordinates. This controversy reveals above all a change in the German intellectual landscape within which Sloterdijk had irrevocably taken his place. Chapter 5 provides an impressionistic portrait of Sloterdijk's panoply of therapeutic prescriptions. This pharmakon, supportive of an alter-modernity, oscillates between a re-enactment of Epicurean retreat, recreating the enclosure of a healthy, sustainable microcity, on the one hand, and the virtues of strong belonging, undermining the supremacy of bourgeois, bellicose, and greedy subjectivity, on the other. The book's conclusion adds a couple of nuances to the portrait of Sloterdijk's work by situating it within the framework of serene observation and serendipity.

Sloterdijk is the creator of a corpus whose raison d'être is to prevent the disappearance of philosophy's *eros* to the sole benefit of scholarly sobriety. Even though he severely criticizes social democracy and the idea of social equality, he deplores the rarefaction of the public's role in philosophy as the perpetual questioning of conventional wisdom. As such, his work shows us that this Nietzsche of the biotech era wants paradoxically to philosophize in the street in the heart of the city and amid his fellow citizens, even if doing so means suffering the occasional rebuke: "Philosophers have only flattered society in various ways; what is important now is to provoke it."[12]

1

Psychopolitics

"Every critique is pioneering work on the pain of the times (*Zeitschmerz*) and a piece of exemplary healing" (CCR xxxvi). In *Critique of Cynical Reason* and intermittently throughout the corpus of his work, Sloterdijk casts himself as a *Zeitdiagnostiker*, a "specialist physician of the pathologies of the opinion apparatus" (ZT 22). In this self-assigned role, he seeks to decode the prevailing mental illnesses of his time and to prescribe a cure for the consequences of having overlooked the diagnosis. In this chapter, the three symptoms analyzed – cynicism, mobilization, and rage – correspond to the following psychopolitical works: *Critique of Cynical Reason*, *Eurotaoismus*, and *Rage and Time*.[1] Before examining these works, it is important to tease out the Nietzschean epistemological horizon of Sloterdijk's psychopolitical approach.

Psychopolitics as rejection of historicism

Sloterdijk's psychopolitical inquiry emerges out of his doctoral thesis on autobiographical narratives in the Weimar Republic.[2] He describes these life stories as a "form of social praxis" (LOL 6) that reveal the mental structure of a state of society via the so-called subjective *and* objective outpourings of individuals. Psychopolitics thus assumes that psychological moods are qualities that can be transferred from individuals to collectivities and vice versa. This transference (*Übertragung*), taken from the vocabulary of psychoanalysis, is, moreover, at the very heart of Sloterdijk's relationship with time and space and with stories and territories that he synchronizes or superposes by means of transmigration.

These processes were also explored in *Der Zauberbaum* (*The Magic Tree*), Sloterdijk's one and only novel. At the book's end, the protagonist Jan van Leyden, an assistant to the hypnotist Marquis de Puységur at the time of the French Revolution, enters the body of Sigmund Freud in his Berggasse office in Vienna (ZB 318–22). This allusion to the fantasies of occultism is not coincidental, insofar as it exemplifies one aspect of Sloterdijk's particular talent and frivolity, when he sets about aligning significant cultural moments with one another and inserting himself into them as a key author. It is worth recalling in this regard that he wrote the preface to *Critique of Cynical Reason* in the summer of 1981 on the occasion of the bicentenary of Kant's *Critique of Pure Reason* (CCR xxx), that his novel on the "discovery of psychoanalysis in 1785"[3] was uncoincidentally published in 1985, and that it was he who was chosen by the Nietzsche-Archiv to give a talk at Weimar on August 25, 2000, the hundredth anniversary of the death of Nietzsche (NA). It was this same Nietzsche who was the first philosopher to be discussed in the *Critique of Cynical Reason* (CCR xxvii–xxix), the first to whom Sloterdijk dedicated a scholarly book (TS), and whom he still defends with the utmost ardour and clarity.[4]

Psychopolitical transference seeks to draw out homologous mental structures among epochs and times far removed from one another. Nietzsche's imprint in this regard will be discussed later. For the moment, however, it is worth noting that Sloterdijk's psychopolitics postulates the synchronicity of certain periods when their moods are concordant with one another. History is neither a continuous nor a discontinuous series of mental or cultural states. Rather, it is a serpentine air duct able to establish contact, via improbable airlocks, between atmospheres accidentally separated in time.

In a short text with the strange though revealing title "Weimar and California,"[5] Sloterdijk argues that psychopolitics inserts itself as a cure for the omnipotence of the historicism that saturated Germany in the 1970s, because this rebirth of the philosophy of history was unfit to serve as a "therapeutic compensation for collective identity crises."[6] The reason, notes Sloterdijk, is that modern philosophies of history (liberalism, Hegelianism, and Marxism) are unable to answer the vital questions: "Who are we really and how should we live?"[7] Because of this failure, he links the mood of the Weimar Republic to that of California in the 1980s. The public's widespread infatuation with a vocabulary of crisis – including pain, loss, social decadence, mistrust of the world, denegation, restoration, and escape into the absolutely new – appears to call upon the same solution in both cases, namely, "dissonance and emptiness" and hurried patchworks of new syntheses that annihilate critical thought.[8] The danger here is that these climates could ultimately foster the increased importance of fatal charismatic figures "as if our own past flowed once again towards us."[9]

Sloterdijk is not speaking as an historian but on behalf of an art form – that of the historical virtuoso – able to attain the "suprahistorical" dimension that Nietzsche prescribed as the cure for the excesses of the science of history. In his *Untimely Meditations*, Nietzsche argues that historicism is hostile to life and youth, that is, to the creative instinct of art: "In producing this effect, history is the antithesis of art: and only if history can endure to be transformed into a work of art will it perhaps be able to preserve instincts or even evoke them."[10] Sloterdijk fully subscribes to Nietzsche's diagnosis and wholly endorses the idea that life is prey to forces contrary to its vital impulse: "It is sick with many illnesses and not only with the memory of its chain – what chiefly concerns us here is that it is suffering from the *malady of history*. Excess of history has attacked life's plastic powers, it no longer knows how to employ the past as a nourishing food."[11]

For Nietzsche and Sloterdijk, this looming evil can be countered only by the hardiness of the historical virtuoso, who becomes the hero through whom art and history are reunited in the suprahistorical. This virtuoso "has developed in himself such a tenderness and susceptibility of feeling that nothing human is alien to him; the most various ages and persons continue to sound in kindred notes on the strings of his lyre."[12] Going to the heart of Sloterdijk's light-hearted and creative relationship with the seriousness of the discipline of history, this passage helps us to understand why he would rather explore the passageways and other airlocks between and among epochs and why he allows himself to fold space and annihilate time.

In sum, psychopolitics is a fully Nietzschean undertaking that, in light of Sloterdijk's foundational inquiry into cynicism, would make Nietzsche a very timely author, given that, in 1874, he had already written: "[t]he oversaturation of an age with history . . . leads [it] into a dangerous mood of irony in regard to itself and subsequently into the even more dangerous mood of cynicism."[13]

Cynicism

"Cynicism is *enlightened false consciousness*. It is that modernized, unhappy consciousness, on which enlightenment has laboured both successfully and in vain" (CCR 5). *Critique of Cynical Reason* is a composite book (26 chapters and 10 excursuses accompanied by 40 illustrations) that presents itself as a study of mores and mentalities. It is Sloterdijk's fundamental psychopolitical work and for this reason must be discussed at length here, all the more so since it is reviewed and amended in his subsequent works. In it, he provides a critical review of the Enlightenment, which, he argues, has not led to the promised emancipation. The spectrum of this review ranges from the darkest to the lightest and most glowing tones as Sloterdijk seeks to separate the best from the worst in the 200-year-old tradition of criticism. The thesis of this eclectic work maintains that late modernity has given birth to the most advanced modern subject – the cynic – faced with whom the usual devices of critique – unmasking, education, dialogue – are caught off guard. As enlightened false consciousness, cynicism breaks the candid conditions of the Enlightenment's pacifying dialogue, for which the autonomy of the subject necessarily comes about through the elimination of ignorance and illusion.[14]

What Kant sought to accomplish in the field of epistemology, politics would seek to accomplish via the state. Indeed, as Sloterdijk notes, the inaugural scenes of modern political thought (in Hobbes, Locke, and Rousseau) were equally absorbed with the problem of self-preservation (*Selbsterhaltung*). However, this seemingly banal imperative carried within it an intrinsically bellicose and paranoid dimension that fueled the development of modern cynicism. Sloterdijk argues that this new form of realism stems less from the desire for emancipation through accurate knowledge of the world (Kant) than from the fear of being deceived or overpowered (Descartes):

> In his proof through doubt Descartes goes as far as the monstrous consideration that perhaps the entire world of appearance is only the work of a *genius malignus*, calculated to deceive us. The emergence of the enlightening, insightful perspective on reality cannot be comprehended without a thorough cooling down of the ego–world relation, without the deep penetration of suspicion and feat about self-preservation to the very roots of modern will to know. (CCR 330)

Taken as the starting point for modern subjectivity, this fear of being deceived, which entails resorting to deception for the purposes of self-preservation, was already in the orbit of cynicism. In the logic of psychopolitical transference, once this presumed inherent impetus of the individual is transferred to the state through the social contract, suspicion and aggression are then deployed on an unprecedented, gigantic, and destructive scale. The self-preservation imperative (and its inherent tendency to be suspicious, hostile, and aggressive) thus reaches the ultimate form of its pathology with general espionage and the worldwide proliferation of atomic bombs.

The enlightened-but-false paradox is thus no mere play on words. If the Enlightenment founders on the rocks of cynicism, it is because "its falseness is already reflexively buffered" (CCR 5). The political subject of emancipation is no longer interested in freeing itself. Knowing that one is mistaken but continuing all the same has become the cynic's maxim for life: "Psychologically, present-day cynics can be understood as borderline melancholics, who can keep their symptoms of depression under control and can remain more or less able to work" (CCR 5). Sloterdijk sees in this state of affairs the symptoms of a dominant mood, of a new "discontent in our culture" (CCR 3) that stands in the way of the naive, optimistic Enlightenment. This warning is all the more alarming inasmuch as he sees it as a point of comparison between the Weimar Republic and the zeitgeist of the 1980s. He argues that from a suprahistorical perspective, the two periods are characterized by the same obsessive attraction to catastrophe, or catastrophilia, the same schizoid morality, and the same desire to deceive and be deceived, "as if our own past flowed once again towards us."

Before examining these mechanisms, it should be noted that *Critique of Cynical Reason* is also an (im)personal account of the disillusionment experienced by the 1968 generation and its attendant profusion of dropouts. As he told his old friend Rüdiger Safranski at their 1981 meeting, at a time when he "vibrate[d] with gentle determination,"[15] Sloterdijk wanted to make his return from Poona (see the introduction) the occasion for a study of the spirit of the times. Finding himself suddenly re-immersed in European psychopolitics, the mechanism of which appeared to him with a new clarity, he also indicated that this book began to write itself following a fortuitous contact with Hannah Arendt's jovial insolence.[16] Taking his experience as material and making his autobiography a field of experimentation, his thinking was thus based on the clash between the Ptolemaic worldview (the spiritual peace of oriental wisdom) and the starkly contrasting Copernican imperative of modern mobilization he experienced following his return (see SV and KMPA). This clarity of vision, coupled with his desire to produce a work far removed from academic specialization and self-censorship, nevertheless represented a serious contribution to the issue of the relationship between fascism and modernity, while offering a few instances of exemplary healing.

Cynicism as fascism: Hitler

A psychopolitical explanation of the rise of fascism does not emphasize the socio-political origins of this tragedy in its analysis. Rather, it seeks answers to the following two questions: What kind of subjectivity fostered the emergence of fascism? What kind of subject is the most easily seduced by Nazism? The issue is a serious one, and Sloterdijk ambitiously sets his sights on grappling with it:

> A critique of cynical reason would remain an academic glass bead game if it did not pursue the connection between the problem of survival and the danger of fascism. In fact, the question of "survival," of self-preservation and self-assertion, to which all cynicisms provide answers, touches on the very central problem of holding the fort and planning for the future in modern nation-states. Through various approaches, I attempt to fix the logical locus of German fascism in the convolutions of modern, self-reflective cynicism. (CCR 8)

This latter clarification is especially important because, in contrast to an entire historiographical approach that establishes and documents the specificity and singularity of Nazism and its crimes against humanity,[17] Sloterdijk seeks rather to reflect upon the close relationship between Nazism and modernity in order to link the German path to the modern one, and vice versa. In this connection, his position is not far removed from those of Heidegger and Schmitt, who also believed that what was German was modern, and that what was modern was German. The former linked modernity to the issues of technology,[18] whereas the latter linked it to issues related to sovereignty.[19]

For Sloterdijk, it is the sickness of modern cynicism left to its own devices that can lead to the idols of fascism. If the Weimar Republic provided the right climate for the generalization of cynicism as a mentality, it was precisely because it was the ideal type of a society made up of "people who realize that the times of naïveté are gone" (CCR 5). It depicted itself via a discourse of crisis and of disintegration, which bordered on catastrophilia: "a sympathy with the catastrophic, the apocalyptic, and the violently spectacular" (CCR 120). But what the Weimar Republic accustomed its citizens to the most was fraud. "Fraud and expectations of being defrauded became epidemic in it" (CCR 483). In this Republic, which was a Reich, con men were fascinating because they accomplished what they set out to do (cheat to win) while revealing that their own cynicism was that of society as a whole: "[They] invent criminal variants of what is [*sic*] officially called careers" (CCR 486). Yet this fascination with the chaotic generalization of false bottoms and double standards paves the way for movements of simplification that promise "the most energetic return to 'substantial' and reliable states of affairs" (CCR 483). It is through this desire to fill the dissonance and the void that cynicism reaches its paroxysm.

"The Weimar Republic may be understood as an age of a universal dawning of reflection, insofar as at that time, such tactics and theories of artfulness and of 'simplicity with duplicity' were developed on all levels" (CCR 490). In the final chapters of *Critique of Cynical Reason*, Sloterdijk gathers together the pieces of his puzzle, juxtaposing the modernization of the lie and autosuggestion with the historical events that brought about the end of the Weimar Republic, which was already a Reich. It is through the lens of these phenomena that he introduces the decisive figure of Hitler. This popular, cynical politician understands that one first has to believe one's own lies through autosuggestion and playacting: "Hitler's recipe is therefore: First, simply, then repeatedly . . . The suggestion, however, begins in the politicians themselves, and their own consciousness is the first addressee of suggestive persuasion" (CCR 489). Hitler was not the only one to play this game. Indeed, as Sloterdijk points out, one of the most popular therapies in the Weimar Republic was the Coué method, the vocabulary of which became commonplace in the popular imagination (CCR 490). In the case of Hitler, this art attained the dimensions of the entire political sphere:

> He knew how to handle the collective will to illusion by creating the backdrops before which the people could let themselves be deceived to their heart's desire. The illusion into which the one who is ready to be deceived thinks of falling will serve the defrauded one simultaneously as an excuse and, in the end, as an explanation [of] why everything had to happen as it did. (CCR 528)

From the perspective of a psychopolitical approach, the why of Hitler's rise stems from a set of causes that can be summarized as follows: the refusal of dissonance and the void goes hand in hand with an appetite for simplifying worldviews and generating sympathy for catastrophe. The acme of cynical consciousness is that of actively alienating oneself and believing in one's own falseness. It is also the culmination of Sloterdijk's dystopian narrative of the state of society in which cynicism holds the reins of power. This said, in the myriad causes, accidents, and learned calculations that put an end to the Weimar Republic, we can also note the role of the movement's key intellectuals. If the captains of the steel industry bought into the idea of Hitler the chancellor, it was "because they believe[d] that one ha[d] to go along with the Hitler course in order to be able to hold onto the course of history" (CCR 526–7) and because a certain Carl Schmitt (a name overlooked by Sloterdijk in his first bestiary of cynics) sold them the idea of a total state, a concept that would serve to justify their support for the Führer.[20]

If we reframe Sloterdijk's contribution to the history of the Weimar Republic, it has to be admitted that it is not a particularly novel idea to claim that the bourgeoisie stood to gain in gambling on the Nazis. Indeed, it had already been anticipated and diagnosed by the Frankfurt School. In his archaeology of the bourgeois era, Horkheimer, using a vocabulary similar to that of Sloterdijk, also talks about a kind of rampant cynicism beginning in 1936:

> Coldness and alienness are the direct result of this basic structure of the epoch: nothing in the essence of the bourgeois individual opposes the repression and annihilation of one's fellow human beings. On the contrary, the circumstance that in this world each becomes the other's competitor, and that even with increasing social wealth there are increasingly too many people, gives the typical individual of the epoch a character of coldness and indifference, one that is satisfied with the most pitiful rationalizations of the most monstrous deeds as long as they correspond to his interest.[21]

This "pitiful rationalization" characterizes with considerable exacti-
tude these schizoid mental states that Sloterdijk richly itemizes in *Critique of Cynical Reason* (military cynicism, sexual cynicism, medical
cynicism, and religious cynicism). Doing with one hand (economics)
what the other hand does not see (morality) is one of the many cynical
scissions imposed by bourgeois society. Sloterdijk is also not the only
one to have employed the lens of critical theory to analyze the period
extending from the 1920s to the 1980s, up to developments that contradicted the essence of modern emancipation. To conclude this section,
mention must be made of Jean-François Lyotard, who also left his mark
by introducing cynicism into the area of academic knowledge.[22] Rather
than coming to the aid of modern ideals of justice, truth, and universal
education, postmodern science legitimates itself through its power to
maximize the input/output ratio, that is, its ability to efficiently support
economic production. Lyotard argues that university authorities have
perfectly internalized this legitimacy shift and that they control and
frame scientific practice through methods that no longer appeal to
rational arguments or truth, but that are based solely on a logic of
power and "utility," a form of cynicism referred to here as
performativity.

Of philosopher dogs and nightingales: Diogenes and Heine

The cynicism in question up to now is that of the elite. *Critique of Cynical
Reason* stands apart from other reviews of modernity's dark figures in
the early 1980s because it offers an infrahistorical collection of expres-
sions, thoughts, and lifestyles that are opposed to and resist the self-
destructiveness of modern cynicism. In contrast to the pessimistic
diagnosis that holds most of Sloterdijk's attention, the book offers a
therapeutic avenue (a pharmakon) that can be represented and summarized in three points: kynicism, centauric writing, and moving
beyond the Frankfurt School.

Kynicism In the history of ideas, ancient cynicism was part of the
family of Athenian schools, alongside Platonism, Aristotelianism, Stoi-
cism, Epicureanism, and skepticism. Notwithstanding their differences
and quarrels with one another, each of these schools claimed Socrates
as its founder. Socrates, who urged us to live according to what we
think, was a source of inspiration to both an elitist current (Plato, Aristotle) that advocated living according to the good, and to a more readily
accessible and consumable plebeian one (Epicurus, Zeno of Citium)
that defined the art of living well. At a time when Athens was awash
with rival doctrines, a colorful figure, a kind of Socrates gone mad,
advocated a return to things themselves by proposing nothing more
than simply living.

That individual was Diogenes of Sinope (*c*.404–323 BC), the so-called human dog and one of the most influential figures of ancient cynicism. Although none of his writings has survived, the testimonials and stories about his life are filled with the themes that underlie his thought. By returning to cynicism's inaugural expression, Sloterdijk insists on keeping the canine etymological root of the Greek *kynikos* (dog-like) by using neologisms such as *kynical* and *kynicism* in discussing the morality and temperament of Diogenes, the philosopher that bites.[23] This distinction between cynicism and kynicism is not merely semantic. It serves as a systematic opposition between the latter's critical and unredeemable impulse and the former's calculating coldness, which adapts itself to societal illusions as long as they correspond to its interest. Diogenes' primal and aggressive kynicism is a plebeian antithesis to idealism, whereas modern cynicism – that of the elite – is a "cheekiness that has changed sides" (CCR 110). It is a cynicism of parvenus who immunize themselves against critique by the kynicism of pariahs. When the pillars of the temple occasionally tremble as a result of the proud autarchy of the kynics, this threat is swamped by the laughter of those who protect hegemonies.[24] Sloterdijk argues that the unhappy, mocking temperament of modern cynicism breaks with the joviality and insolence of kynicism, as well as with its powerfully critical stance against all hypocrisies raised to the status of social norms:

> Ancient cynicism, at least in its Greek origins, is in principle cheeky. In its cheekiness lies a method worthy of discovery. This [method] is viewed unjustly, beside the great systems in Greek philosophy – Plato, Aristotle, the Stoa – as a mere game of satyrs, as a half-jovial, half-dirty episode, and is passed over. In *kynismos* a kind of argumentation was discovered that, to the present day, respectable thinking does not know how to deal with. (CCR 101)

Diogenes is the prototypical dropout. He lived in a barrel lying against the walls of Athens, offering up to his "civilized" fellow citizens the performance art of someone who depended on nothing and no one. His radical asceticism was inspired by natural models (*physis*): the dog that bites anyone who disturbs his kennel, the mouse that lives off the scraps of civilization, and the child that drinks with her hands. He opposed these models of a frugal, undomesticated life to the artifices of culture (*nomos*) and the misfortunes of vulgar imbeciles or sophisticated philosophers who accept the hold of social conventions over their lives and their bodies. In addition to mocking Plato, whose aristocratic origins and pedantry he never failed to point out, Diogenes shocked those around him by defecating, urinating, masturbating, and fornicating in public. The legendary Diogenes was even visited by Alexander the Great, who asked him what he desired. Diogenes replied "Stop blocking my sun."[25]

What is philosophical about the bare life led by Diogenes? In what way is his scabrous and irreverent behaviour a form of *argument*? In his sympathetic depiction of Diogenes, Sloterdijk replies that it is a form of argument through "pantomimic materialism" (CCR 103), that is, the speech act of the clown who uses his or her body as a vehicle of satirical expression as well as a criterion of truth: "Here begins a laughter containing philosophical truth, which we must call to mind again if only because today everything is bent on making us forget how to laugh" (CCR 106). In the long history of psychopolitics, the kynical impulse resurfaces whenever high theory neglects the life of the body and perpetuates a schizoid image of civilization erected on the basis of a fallacious revealed/hidden, clean/dirty, public/private dichotomy. Kynical gestures are a reappropriation of the body, of which no one should be ashamed.[26] More importantly, as a view looking from below up to cynicisms on high, the kynical position is well placed to negotiate an uninhibited relationship with truth and candid speaking (*parrhesia*):

> From this perspective, the significance of cheekiness is easily shown. Since philosophy can only hypocritically live out what it says, it takes cheek to say what is lived. In a culture in which hardened idealisms make lies into a form of living, the process of truth depends on whether people can be found who are aggressive and free ("shameless") enough to speak the truth. (CCR 102)

As a sign of the times or of the transmigration of ideas, kynicism's parrhesiastic capacity was also at the heart of Foucault's last course at the Collège de France in the winter of 1984.[27] Within their respective projects, both Foucault and Sloterdijk feel that these hardened idealisms are the ancient counterpart to contemporary cynicism – the cynicism of the elite – against which stands the courageous parrhesiastic act.

Ultimately, kynicism formulates an existential choice between acceptance and refusal to participate in a schizophrenic society, what Sloterdijk refers to as the alternative "between embodiment or splitting" (CCR 120). Kynical embodiment chooses to live and, true to the Enlightenment's first steps, it chooses a conscious life: "It unfolds in a broad field of individuals and groups who carry on the kynical impulse and who attempt what no politics and no mere art can take from them: to tackle, with their alertness, the splits and unconscious elements that seep into individual existence" (CCR 120).

The centauric art of writing   Kynical satire is also one of the critical weapons used in the early days of the Enlightenment. "Here it becomes clearer than anywhere that 'philosophical' ideology critique is truly the heir of a great *satirical* tradition" (CCR 16). Prior to the generalization of the model of a professorial career and the seriousness of academic institutions, the literary forms of the critique of power were both varied and permissive: laughter, making faces, caricature, novels, plays, philosophical treatises, encyclopaedias, etc. Sloterdijk argues that the stagnant state of contemporary critique can be explained by the forgotten nature of this kynical heritage, that is, "the powerful traditions of laughter in satirical knowledge" (CCR 16). Yet the rediscovery of the joy of critique requires a re-engagement with the strength of this impulse. The same is true for the Enlightenment: "[it] can gain a new lease on life and remain true to its most intimate project: the transformation of being through consciousness" (CCR 82).

Heine, Marx, Nietzsche, and Freud were major propagators of this satire capable of thought and of this "holy non-seriousness, which remains one of the sure indexes of truth" (CCR 18). At the beginning of *Critique of Cynical Reason*, it is with the first of these authors that Sloterdijk wishes to associate himself.[28] As such, in addition to the dog's bites, Sloterdijk wants to borrow from the nightingale's song, the symbol from Romantic literature that incarnates the disturbing strangeness of the world, the desire for the sublime, and the aversion to the useful.[29] In this regard, Heine gives us a delectable story about the nightingale that disturbed the quietude of clerics and monks:

> On the tree perched a nightingale, which was rejoicing and sobbing in the tenderest and most melting melodies. As they listened, the learned doctors felt wondrously happy; the warm, spring-like notes pierced the scholastic defences of their hearts, their feeling woke from their dull hibernation, they looked at one another with astonishment and delight. At last one of them made the astute observation that something peculiar was happening, that the nightingale might well be a devil, which was trying to distract them with its lovely sounds from their Christian conversations, and seduce them into sensual enjoyment and other sweet sins; and he began an exorcism . . . To this conjuration, it is said, the bird replied: "Yes, I am an evil spirit!" and flew away laughing.[30]

Heine's cruel non-seriousness and his ability to treat serious matters with light-heartedness influenced the young Marx of the 1840s and earned the admiration of Freud[31] and Nietzsche before him.[32] Following the publication of Sloterdijk's novel, the capacity for truth in literature was an approach at the heart to his first essay on Nietzsche. The meeting of art and philosophy is depicted in this work in terms of centauric literature, "that is, the setting loose of an infinitely consequential artistic and philosophical double-natured eloquence" (TS 10).[33] Initially, Sloterdijk viewed this centauric tradition as the site of resistance to the professionalization of the act of thinking, that is, to the invasion of the field of knowledge by the cynicism of professional thinkers: "Enlightenment means to affirm all antischizophrenic movements. The universities are scarcely the place where this happens" (CCR 120).

Philosophizing like a dog, singing like a night bird, and accepting that resistance comes from the margin are part of the kynical dropout's heroism that Sloterdijk proposes for reinvigorating the Enlightenment. It would seem in this regard that if Heine was the "nightingale nested in Voltaire's wig,"[34] then Sloterdijk was to become the one who would ruffle the feathers of the Frankfurt School's thinking heads.

With and against the Frankfurt School   Although Sloterdijk initially appeared to identify himself as part of the lineage of the Frankfurt School in his project for reinvigorating the Enlightenment, it was only to lighten the weight of his critical attack against his older teachers. As a child of his times, like many of his contemporaries, he had to deal with the influence of Adorno and Horkheimer's *Dialectic of Enlightenment* (1944).[35] The theme of the Enlightenment deviating from its emancipatory goals imposed itself as a philosophical locus, and it was through this doorway that Sloterdijk made his entrance. However, despite his nuancing, Sloterdijk associated the Frankfurt School itself with the bankruptcy of the Enlightenment because, in his view, it had come to symbolize this spirit of depression and resignation that, in grumbling about the state of the world, drowned the critical approach in a priori pain: "That is the reason for the stagnation of Critical Theory. The offensive manoeuvre of refusing to collaborate has long been ineffective. The masochistic element has outdone the creative element" (CCR, xxxv).

In support of his arguments, Sloterdijk related a series of events that occurred in 1969 to substantiate the idea of a necessarily kynical overthrow of critical theory:

> Shortly before Adorno died there was a scene in a lecture hall at Frankfurt University . . . The philosopher was just about to begin his lecture when a group of demonstrators prevented him from mounting the podium. Such scenes were not unusual in 1969. On this occasion something happened that required a closer look. Among the disrupters were some female students who, in protest, attracted attention to themselves by exposing their breasts to the thinker. Here, on one side, stood naked flesh, exercising "critique"; there, on the other side, stood the bitterly disappointed man without whom scarcely any of those present would have known what critique meant – cynicism in action. It was not naked force that reduced the philosopher to muteness, but the force of the naked.[36] (CCR xxxvii)

In this same month (April 1969), Adorno chose to close the Frankfurt institute forcefully because it was occupied by a sit-in by 76 students (described as left-wing fascists), who were immediately removed by the police. The malaise engendered by this unfortunate episode resonated in correspondence between Marcuse and Adorno. Indeed, Marcuse severely criticized Adorno, clearly overwhelmed by the events, for his repressive actions.[37]

For his part, Sloterdijk preferred to meditate on the philosophical meaning of this kynical feminist provocation. He noted the irony of the situations in which the advocate of entirely theoretical emancipation found himself dispossessed and rendered helpless by the impatient and colorful spectacle of an attempt at emancipation through gestures:

> Ironically, of all people, Adorno, one of the greatest theoreticians of modern aesthetics, fell prey to the neokynical impulse . . . They were, almost in the ancient sense, kynically bared bodies, bodies as arguments, bodies as weapons. Their showing themselves, independently of the private motives of the demonstrators, was an antitheoretical action. In some sort of confused sense, they may have understood their act as a "praxis of social change," in any case, as something more than lectures and intellectual seminars. Adorno, in a tragic but understandable way,
> • has slipped into the position of the idealistic Socrates, and the women into the position of the unruly Diogenes. Against the most insightful theory these – it is to be hoped – intelligent bodies willfully positioned themselves. (CCR 109–10)

This turning of Adorno "on his head" signifies that a genuine critique has to go from the head toward the body.[38] In this vein, the inescapable Adornian moment – suffering from a *mal du siècle* – must be superseded by the state of felicity of a gay science. Above and beyond the telling of these stories, we also learn that genuine critique comes from elsewhere, that healing must take other paths, and that the intellectual and emotional resources of updated critical thinking are to be found elsewhere than in Frankfurt. To this end, Sloterdijk not only calls upon centauric authors or neokynical heroines, he also goes so far as to hijack the source of critique so as to reinstate it within the framework of its genuine tradition against the Frankfurt School's "monopoly." The discreet master-thinker came out of his lair: one cannot think in new ways about the world without *also* counting on Heidegger.

> Without knowing it and, for the most part, even without wanting to know it (in this country even with an outraged resoluteness not to recognize it), the New Left is an existential Left, a neokynical Left – I risk the expression: a *Heideggerian Left*. This is, particularly in the land of Critical Theory, which has hung an almost impenetrable taboo on the "fascist" ontologist, a rather piquant discovery. (CCR 209)

Although Sloterdijk discreetly lifts up his mask as he steps off stage after the first act, what cannot be read here is the programmatic formula of this hypothesis, which would become the new philosopher's signature. What cannot *as yet* be read here is the death of critical theory.[39]

Mobilization

This long journey within the psychopolitics of cynicism has enabled a discussion of the fundamental themes of the young Sloterdijk's thought, which have continued to hold his attention in subsequent works: catastrophilia; fascism and modernity; and the therapeutic means for escaping this continuum of self-destruction. In *Eurotaoismus*,[40] Sloterdijk extends the psychopolitics of *Critique of Cynical Reason* and studies the modern mobility pathology on the basis of Ernst Jünger's diagnosis and a therapeutic approach still identified with Heidegger.[41] In keeping with his imagistic approach, the book is filled with a rich iconography that serves as a subtext meant to explain the modern obsession with infinite mobility: ads for airlines, cars, athletic shoes, banks, military campaigns, escalators, space probes, Saturn's rings, etc. Since Copernicus, modern cosmology has not only distanced itself from the ancient idea of a fixed cosmos and its accompanying worldview, it has also made kinetics modernity's ethical criterion par excellence. Indeed, this criterion goes so far as to convince modern human beings that where they have come to a halt, they have lost their freedom. In this new instance of a psychopolitical analysis of modern times, Sloterdijk succinctly presents the three "axioms" that serve as points of departure for his critique of kinetics: "First, that we are moving in a world that is moving itself; second, that the self-movements of the world include our own self-movements and affect them; and third, that in modernity, the self-movements of the world originate from our self-movements, which are cumulatively added to world-movement" (ET 30).[42]

This movement toward movement goes hand in hand with the ideal of autonomy lying at the heart of modernity: this "self-igniting self-movement without which modernity would not exist" (ET 36).[43] In its progressive idealization, this forward movement has been described as being fully under the control of the enlightened, informed, and far-sighted subject. However, this optimism of progress is no longer in phase with the customary catastrophes of late modernity (as attested by, for example, the 1986 explosion of the nuclear power plant in Chernobyl), and it is for this reason that the self-initiating subject of modernity must also be seen as an actor who is the subject of his or her own actions.

It is from the anti-modern perspective that Sloterdijk identifies the clearest diagnoses of the evils he wishes to analyze. He refers firstly to the Romantic poet Novalis and to the "self-grinding mill" metaphor that he uses to critique modern disenchantment and its questioning of European Christianity. This perpetual motion – which sadly shows Novalis to be right – engenders a dual "endogenous self-movement and exogenous external movement" that lead the modern "I" "into mindlessness, catastrophe, loss of inhibition, death" (ET 41).[44] It is thus in a rather sombre way that Sloterdijk announces his central argument: "That which first appeared to be a controlled departure towards freedom has turned out to be a slide into catastrophic and uncontrollable heteromobility" (ET 24). To put it in more brutal terms, "nothing happens as expected" (ET 24), since movement is controlled only by movement.

In framing the problem in this way, Sloterdijk dispenses with modern, progressive discourse (which he calls naive and optimistic) and turns to the few authors who have coldly and objectively examined the proliferation of self-mobility and heteromobility throughout the world. It is at this precise moment in his argument that Sloterdijk introduces the concept of mobilization, as developed by Jünger in his 1932 book *Der Arbeiter (The Worker)*.[45] Well aware that the term *mobilization* was part of the vocabulary of war and that Jünger had been suspected of being a fascist, Sloterdijk nevertheless respects "the cold optic of the analysis" and its "perceptiveness" (ET 50).[46] Indeed, if, oddly enough, military theorists such as Jünger and even Schmitt have to be evoked, claims Sloterdijk, it is because they point in the direction of the modern malaise and because mobilization and its warmongering overtones might well awaken our anxiety. Jünger's *The Worker* refers to:

> the planetary subject of mobilization, trembling from working out, hardened from pain, the neo-objective high-performance type in his decided mission for the action system that is exalting itself, arming itself, throwing itself to the front, also called the progressive action system (whether we mean a firm, class, people, nation, block, or state of the world is irrelevant on this level of action).[47] (ET 50)

This militaro-productive figure obeys the maxim of total performance.[48] In chapters 2 and 4, the Exercising (*Übender*) and Achiever (*Leistungsträger*) figures will be contrasted with what Sloterdijk views here as "disturbing and destructive." For the moment, let us remain on the path leading from diagnosis to therapy on the one hand and good and bad mobility on the other.

Planes, trains, and automobiles

To the extent that it has reached a cosmological status, movement for movement's sake can be found in every aspect of civilization. To make the Copernican cosmos explicit in the day-to-day world of transportation, it suffices to reflect upon the automobile and to study this machine as an anthropologist would: "Whoever is driving an automobile is approaching the divine; he feels how his diminutive I is expanding into a higher self that offers us the whole world of highways as a home and that makes us realize that we are predestined to a life beyond the animal-like life of pedestrians" (ET 42).[49] However, this promise of general mobility collides with its exact opposite (immobility) and has an unpleasant consequence. Without yet speaking in terms of a catastrophe, we can speak of this other face of the control that people experience by themselves, to wit, the traffic jam, the very failure of automobility:

> Such situations represent the failure of fake modernity, the end of an illusion – like a kinetic Good Friday when all hope for redemption by acceleration is lost. On these glowing hot afternoons . . . dark thoughts rise into the air just like black exhaust fumes; drivers gain historical-philosophical insight; critical words for civilization pronounced in glossolalia escape their lips; the obituaries of modernity blow out of the side windows; whatever school degree the drivers have, they come to the conclusion that it cannot go on like this for much longer. A foreshadowing of another "era." Even those who have never heard of the term postmodernity are already familiar with the thing itself on such afternoons in a traffic jam. And in fact, this can be formulated in terms of cultural theory: where unleashed self-movement leads to a halt or a whirl, the beginning of a transitional experience emerges, in which the modern active changes to the postmodern passive.[50] (ET 43)

Not at all convinced by the pompous discourse of postmodern theories that devotes itself much more to reconciliation than to condemnation, Sloterdijk prefers to think about the catastrophe continuum by drawing on concrete experiences. From the automobility that has become static, he shifts to the atomic level of movement: the chain reaction of mobility, this other form of induced and harnessed mobilization that is under the control not of a modern "I" but of the evil genius of the unforeseen and the incalculable. From Harrisburg (Pennsylvania) in 1979 to Chernobyl (Ukraine) in 1986, overheating or exploding reactors have entered into a popular imagination that has become accustomed to catastrophe (ET 102–12).[51] In terms of the catastrophilia characteristic of the 1980s, *Eurotaoismus* and *Critique of Cynical Reason* can be viewed as twin works in which catastrophe has lost its pedagogical value. The idea of learning from one's mistakes is a maxim that has been eclipsed by the cynical advocates of mobilization, who well know that we are in danger but lead us into it all the same:

> In these communities, there are mentalities that are massively and irreversibly specialized in mobilization, and these mentalities resist all

disturbances in the bunker of their reflexes. The evidence of catastrophe, even that which is genuinely present, slides over these structures. For them, the revelation does not take place. Ultimately, consciousnesses are harder than facts, and the one that, formerly, did not want to listen to advice (when it was still possible to do so) will now also refuse, at its expense, to educate itself. (ET 112)

As such, a critique of mobilization is searching for a posture that side-steps the imperative to be in motion.

A critical theory of being-in-the-world

What Sloterdijk subtly announced, in his initial critique of cynicism, as a project aimed at renewing the Enlightenment appears much more clearly here as a project of abandonment. In looking to Romantics and proto-fascist thinkers for a point of departure for his critical reflections, he profanes legitimate usages and patronages. In other words, the bankruptcy of the Frankfurt School or, for that matter, institutionalized academia is no longer viewed with reticence. *Eurotaoismus* has as its focus modernity *and* critical theory itself because neither of them is able to tease out a critical horizon of mobilization. In his quest, Sloterdijk looks for a theoretical language that can find refuge neither in ancient metaphysics nor in the inverted celebration of movement for move-ment's sake, but in the creative fusion of streams and intuitions that until now have been distinct from one another:

> A critique of this kind prevents cynico-melancholic grounding in a world that now presents itself everywhere as postmodern consent. But it also avoids masochistic contemplation of the totality that leads to metaphys-ical marginalism. Neither against the refusal to engage itself nor in agree-ment, the objective of alternative critique is to promote a critical theory of being-in-the-world. (ET 13)

Adorno *plus* Heidegger: Sloterdijk pleads for a fusion of critical theory and phenomenology. In revisiting Frankfurt via Freiburg, Sloterdijk reveals his preferences and advances the idea that Freiburg is in fact the real seat of a critique of modern mobilization. To critique false "mobilized, enlightened consciousness"[52] is to define modern mobili-zation as, in principle, the world's destructive impulse. In place of the ancient metaphysical hatred of the triviality of the day-to-day world, a global elite is spreading a nihilism of the volatilization of all that inhabits the surface of the globe. In searching for an outside point of view, that of a non-participant, it is Heidegger who, according to Slo-terdijk, adopts this discourse from a small hut in the mountains of the Black Forest.[53] In this Copernican world, Heidegger had an outside-looking-in point of view that embraced the site of being human, the pathway of a "theory of birth, a phenomenology of coming-into-the-world [*Zurweltkommens*]" (ET 194).

Sloterdijk not only designates himself as a new elite here, but also develops an entire research program that would take on the names of "Anthropotechnics" (chapter 2) and "Spherology" (chapter 3) 12 years later. A pharmakon to prevent mobilization calls for an anthropology of the species that enables the birth of the human. This philosophy, whose countours were sketched out in *Eurotaoismus*, would subsequently become one that examined the conditions of preservation of that which preserves.

On rest and Tao

There is no trace of Taoism in this critique of movement, despite the curious admixture announced by the book's title.[54] In the relevant section (the third section of the third part), we can read the following: "the EuroTao that can be spoken is not the real EuroTao, etc." (ET 210).[55] Although the book offers up a therapy consisting of the right kind of mobility, this makes its appearance in the final paragraphs and points, rather, in the direction of rest as demobilization:

> The person who knows what nothing else to do means (*nichts mehr zu tun zuhaben*) is the only one who has a criterion of the right kind of mobility. Instead of massive forward mobilization, an entirely mobile, *in loco* suspension becomes possible. The path of critique transforms itself into a critique of the path. (ET 338)

Although Sloterdijk had yet to settle his scores with the Frankfurt School, he no longer wanted to philosophize on the basis of a duty to save modernity. The only worthwhile critique was one that "would establish itself from the very start as a preschool of demobilization [while] everything else is the rational makeup of complicity" (ET 53).[56]

Rage

The 2006 publication of *Rage and Time* took place in a psychopolitical atmosphere perturbed by the events of September 11, 2001, and the collateral multiplication of wars on terror.[57] Although it is too soon to definitively affirm it here, these events and the thoughts to which they gave rise appear to have led to a turning point in Sloterdijk's work.[58] In 2002, while still reeling from these events, he published a first excerpt of *Schäume* (*Foams*) (SIII 89–196) under the title *Terror from the Air*, the German subtitle of which – *An den Quellen des Terrors* (*On the Sources of Terror*) – resonated even more with the editorial pretext provided by

the mood of 9/11.[59] In this work, Sloterdijk did not utter a single word
about Al-Qaeda, George W. Bush, or the World Trade Center. However,
he located the source of twentieth-century terrorism in the use by the
Germans of a deadly gas on the French front in 1915 (TA 9–17). *Atmoter-
rorism* is the name he gave to the birth of the war of extermination:
attacking the enemy's conditions of life – the air – to eradicate them.
This murderous technique and its many gaseous variations (Zyklon-B,
incendiary bombs, napalm, etc.) are accompanied, however, by a pedagogical discovery, to wit, the environment. It is for this reason that this
short essay subsequently reflects upon the ancestry of the techniques
of mastering the air, of air conditioning and the manufacturing of life
or death atmospheres.[60]

It was only after the 2004 publication of the final volume of the
Spheres trilogy and its geo-philosophical counterpart, *In the World Interior of Capital*, the following year that Sloterdijk made public the fruit
of his reflections on the outbreak of anger that was gripping the planet.
Rage and Time was surprising in more ways than one and displeased a
leftist readership for two reasons: firstly, because it a-critically adopted
the arguments of Straussian hawks such as Francis Fukuyama, who,
from his command post in Washington, colored the air breathed in all
of NATO's bunkers;[61] and, secondly, because it surfed on the end-of-
communism discourse and raged at the revolutionary tradition, which
it referred to as pure ressentiment.[62] One thing is certain: Sloterdijk
showed his true colors in the subtle realignment announced in the
book's German subtitle, *Politisch-psychologischer Versuch*, namely that it
was no longer a case of a *psychopolitical* investigation, but of a *politico-
psychological* essay that sought (and herein lies his argument) to
prioritize the virility of the *thymos* of war over the *eros* of rest and
introspection (RT 13–19).[63]

Between *menis* and *thymos*

Menis – the rage of Achilles in the *Iliad* – is the first word of the Western
literary tradition. Sloterdijk argues that the ascendance of this word is
not merely symbolic. It is equally the result of a long history of political
successes in collecting and using rage in the deployment of Western
power (RT 2). The rage of the gods, which for the Hellenics was "an
active force in quintessential shape" (RT 7) and which led to pure,
direct and unhesitating action, has been taken up, if in a somewhat
domesticated way, in a political objective that seeks at once to provoke
and control rage:

> *Menis* belongs to the group of invasive energies. The poetic as well as the
> philosophical psychology of the Hellenics included these energies and
> taught that they were to be considered gifts of grace from the divine

world. Just as every gifted person is asked from above to carefully administer the gift that has been entrusted to him, the hero, the guardian of rage, also has to create a conscious relationship to this rage. (RT 11)

This first shift of eruptive rage toward a conscious relationship and a domesticated, rational use clarifies somewhat the object of Sloterdijk's investigation. Although the title announces a reflection on divine rage, it is, rather, a human-made, derived passion/virtue that lies at the heart of the book.

This controlled, thoughtful, and domesticated rage is called pride or *thymos*. The taming of rage through the organization and valuing of the virtues of thymotic courage has been a task of interest to moral and political thought since Plato. With Plato, the domestication of rage "is situated halfway between worship of quasi-divine Homeric *menis* and the stoic dismissal of wrathful and intensive impulses" (RT 23). In his very brief incursion into book 4 of *The Republic*, Sloterdijk glosses over the fact that Plato inserted *thymos* into a tripartition, and not into a "bipolar dynamics of the human psyche" (RT 23). Indeed, thymotic rage is what Plato brings into play between the rational or calculating part and the desiring part of the psyche, and is what "sets its arms on the side of the calculating part."[64] Rage is experienced whenever the virtuous subject gives into his or her desires,[65] and since the desiring part and the reasoning part are of equal strength, it is the intervention of *thymos* that ensures that reason prevails over desire. For Plato, although rage does have a political potential, it is only to the extent that it is situated within the framework of an ideal order in which rational leaders assisted by the courage of the military come to dominate simple workers. However, Sloterdijk borrows neither Plato's tripartite division of the soul and the city nor his hierarchical vocabulary of political castes, but adopts instead a dualistic understanding of the tensions that pull us one way or the other between an erotic pole and a thymotic one. Before discussing this tension and its accompanying politico-psychological diagnoses, Sloterdijk undertakes a re-reading of the entire evolution of subsequent Western and Christian history from the perspective of the idea of the use of rage in politics.

Among the transmission points of this long narrative, he pays particular attention to the eighteenth century. When it was perhaps least expected, the virtue of blind vengeance, in the midst of the golden age of treatises on education and perpetual peace, became the major justification of the revolutionary culture of the sans-culottes. As such, the pacifying age of Enlightenment led to its opposite: "Since the past is fundamentally always unjust, the inclination increases, not always but with increased regularity, to extol revenge as just" (RT 50). For the next two centuries, the French Revolution inspired the political model of collecting, using, and converting rage via the establishment of a "world

bank of rage," the central leadership of which was subsequently taken
over by advocates of the communist revolution:

> Through the creation of a bank of rage (understood as a storage place for
> moral explosives and vengeful projects) individual vectors become part
> of a single project guided by a single administration, the demands of
> which do not always coincide with the rhythms of local actors and
> actions. But now subjection becomes inevitable: countless histories of
> rage are finally united in one common history. (RT 62)

The banking metaphor used ad nauseam by Sloterdijk (transactions,
accumulations, bonds, etc.) reveals the mechanism that serves as the
book's main thesis. In light of this world collection of compiled stories
about hints of rage, the art of political leadership involves the intelli-
gent use of the accumulated combustible elements of rage, which at
times have to be kindled while at others they have to be restrained:
"On the one hand, this cold-bloodedness constantly needs to stir hatred
and outrage. On the other hand, it is also necessary for securing
restraint" (RT 65–6).

However, this political art that uses dynamite with parsimony went
through a monstrous, genocidal mutation in the communist adventure
of the twentieth century. And even though Western communism has
been critical of the revolution's hijacking by Soviet strong-arm thugs
and their satellites since the earliest writings of Antonio Gramsci and
Rosa Luxemburg, Sloterdijk displays a kind of fury that is curiously
reminiscent of revisionist historians.[66] When the left had regained total
freedom in its re-reading of Marx and was seeking to re-weave the
fabric of an idea of communism,[67] Sloterdijk busied himself instead
with discrediting the entire Jacobin revolutionary tradition since 1789
by linking communism to fascism and by lumping (a bit too quickly,
perhaps) the idea of revolution into the Nietzschean category of *ressentiment*, that is, a "vengeful attitude of inhibited life" (AP 37) that has
neither the pride nor the honor of a well-disciplined *thymos*. It is via
this caricature that he also denigrates some of the emblematic names
of the contemporary left – Negri, Badiou, Žižek – by pointing his ironic
or accusing finger at them.

Of the three, only Žižek appears to have taken Sloterdijk as a serious
adversary, and he returns the irony of the diminishing mirror by accusing Sloterdijk of being a "liberal-conservative who acts like the *enfant
terrible* of contemporary German thought."[68] Underneath it all, however,
the issue is a serious one. For his part, Žižek believes in the value of
Jacobin pedagogy and even of Leninism for the development of resistance in today's world, notwithstanding the worries that moderates
(conservatives or liberals) have about political violence: "perhaps the
time has now come to turn this mantra around and admit that a good

dose of just that 'Jacobin-Leninist' paradigm is precisely what the Left needs today," that we need "strict egalitarian justice, disciplinary terror, political voluntarism, and trust in the people. This matrix is not 'superseded' by any new postmodern or postindustrial or post-whatever-you-want dynamic."[69]

Thymos over *eros*

In Sloterdijk's view, Žižek's wish will not soon be fulfilled, given that the end of the revolutionary tradition led in a confused manner to the disappearance of *thymos* in the Western community. At a more intellectual and conceptual level, the most polemical charge of *Rage and Time* is situated less in the well-traced if not banal field of anti-communism than in psychoanalysis, the assumed source of this discontent in the culture of pride. In the book's final section, although Sloterdijk focuses on the dissipation of *thymos*, even the most attentive reader would get only a vague idea of the therapeutics the *Zeitdiagnostiker* wishes to associate with the evils of this lack.[70]

It is worth recalling that Sloterdijk retains only two of the three terms making up Plato's tripartite division of the soul: *thymos* and *eros*. From Freud, Sloterdijk takes the notion that *eros* designates an insatiable need that must be repressed through education in order to emerge from its infantile narcissism. However, he criticizes the Berggasse doctor for having failed to produce "an analogous educational path for the production of the proud adult, of the fighter, and bearer of ambitions" (RT 14). The neglect of Plato's *thymos* in psychoanalysis has contributed to a loss of dignity in Western culture that has culminated in "contemporary consumerism [which] achieves the same interruption of pride for the sake of eroticism" (RT 16). The binarism used by Sloterdijk is both clear and airtight: "While eroticism points to ways leading to those 'objects' that we lack and whose presence or possession makes us feel complete, thymotics discloses ways for human beings to redeem what they possess, to learn what they are able to do, and to see want they want" (RT 15–16). This opposition is not only exclusive, it is also articulated in a counter-intuitive manner, almost to the point of going against common sense – where *eros* is in need, *thymos*, for its part, has reached plenitude; the latter is in the folds of dignity and generosity whereas the former (still) leads to ressentiment.

Critics of this inversion did not fail to identify the polemical subtext of this charge against emancipation narratives, inspired by the Freudian critique of the social repression of *eros*. Examining matters more closely, do we really live in a society built on the triumph of the erotic, or are we still in the thrall of the capitalism of repressive enjoyment described by Marcuse and Freudo-Marxists?[71] Is this proud, thymotic subject not precisely an outgrowth of the narcissistic age, continually in need of spectators to applaud even its smallest achievement, that is, its world of appearance?[72] If ressentiment is this omnipresent poison spreading throughout post-Christian culture, should we not identify it instead with a domination of asceticism that is the antithesis of the erotic side of things? Are not these undignified adults about whom Sloterdijk speaks in fact the subjects of a control society that represses *eros* and infantilizes the right to smoke, drink, swear, and eat? If Sloterdijk's concern now turns deep down on the realization that "we no longer know how and when to fight,"[73] in what sense does it remain faithful to critical pantomimic materialism and the commandment regarding the reappropriation of the body? Is the politico-psychological inversion the trace of the abandonment of the pacifying emancipation that took the subversive, disarming erotic path? To be sure, while the advocates of a materialist position are well aware "that reactionary forces never come from the erotic pole,"[74] it is not clear whether Sloterdijk has yet to subscribe to this idea. To measure the extent of this contrast, it is worth recalling the tone of the psychopolitical cure developed in *Critique of Cynical Reason*, in which Sloterdijk believed that it was in the interest of the aggressive, conquering subject of modernity to dissolve itself into an erotic relationship to the world: "Only through *eros* do we become capable of conceding the 'object' a precedence. And even if I cease to be, *eros* wills that Something remain" (CCR 361).

In hindsight, we can see that this categorization radically opposing *eros* and *thymos* is in fact not a circumstantial departure from the earlier psychopolitical approach, because that is kept intact throughout the following years. Sloterdijk even makes it a criterion for distinguishing between two kinds of societies: "What we have called 'society' since the Enlightenment is the code name for a community of poly-thematic and mass-media stress. Its internal tone irregularly oscillates between two extreme states: casual entertainment and combative closing of ranks" (RNU 47). The former collective (European style) allows the freedom to enjoy an apolitical life in which its members leave on vacation, whereas the latter (American style) requires its members to stand together and instinctively share the same "Maximal-Stress-Impulse" (RNU 49). Notwithstanding the distance taken or the shift laid out by *Rage and Time*, psychopolitical analysis does not completely disappear from Sloterdijk's diagnostic and therapeutic register (indeed, the notion of political stress is used in *Theory of the Post-War Periods* in speaking about the Franco-German pairing). Above and beyond the political wanderings to which these hawkish diagnoses can lead (chapter 4), there is a therapeutic side to the political economy of *thymos* (which can also take the form of self-reliance and giving as an end in it itself). A more thorough examination of this issue is provided in chapter 5.

2

Anthropotechnics

"Conceptions which stand in opposition to one another are preferably expressed in dreams by the same element."[1] So claims Freud in arguing that dreams overcome their contradictory desires by expressing them via a single symbol. The Freudian conception of dreams and primitive words as beyond good and evil sheds considerable light on the combination of meanings Sloterdijk uses in formulating his concept of *anthropotechnics*. If dreams and primitive words have a double meaning, it is because they are indifferent to the principle of non-contradiction and do not ask us to choose between the round and the square in our attempts to square the circle. However, Freud seeks less to relate the dream's "objective" content than to give omnipotence to the analyzer who, via a narrative, structures this double meaning so as to draw out a single meaning.

Thinking the co-dependence of contraries and uniting them through narrative is the overarching device employed by Sloterdijk in the undertaking explored in this chapter. Sloterdijk becomes an anthropo-technologist and bestows upon himself the title of storyteller of the origins of humanity. This title is worth mulling over because it reveals that the content and form of his undertaking are inseparable. Narrative logic is more effective than argumentative reasoning in drawing out the primitive scene of nascent humanity. The primacy of myth over philosophy and science is not merely a matter of seniority or prestige. It is the perfect way of grasping the intrinsic unity of what has been falsely isolated or opposed. *Anthropotechnics* is a neologism that (re-) merges entities that were already inseparable in primitive times. This anthropodicy that Sloterdijk invites us to consider consists of a rewriting of the nature/culture divide. If this orientation formulates the intuition of an original fusion of humanity and machine, it is because it dissociates itself from the humanist/rationalist tradition. Sloterdijk draws rather on fantastical narratives that rely on a certain degree of fear and irrational fascination. He favors the superiority of this sort of "fantastical reconstructivism" (NG 154) over evolutionist or scientific schools of thought. This narrative is thus a "techno-mytho-logy."[2]

By turning the page on the irresolvable contradictions opposing the artificial to the natural or the innate to the acquired, Sloterdijk is preparing to stir up a few taboos and reveal the meaning he intends to give to his anti/posthumanism.[3] This positioning entails three developments that are the focus of this chapter. Firstly, the humanist educational program is a failure, a state of affairs that requires the emergence of new rulers or breeders. Secondly, humanism's anti-technology paranoia is outdated and the human–technics relation needs to be rewritten. Thirdly, the egalitarian trends of the major humanist systems gloss over or overlook the fact that exceptional individuals can surpass themselves through exercise and restore an athletic, grandiose meaning to self-improvement.

Rules for the Human Zoo

Despite their commercial success, Sloterdijk's essays and the tone characterizing them did not redefine the space of intellection positions until the late 1990s. His increasing extra-academic outbursts and his bringing back into fashion the biting prose of a Heine or a Nietzsche ultimately stirred up a political hornet's nest.

In 1999, Sloterdijk gave a talk titled "Regeln für den Menschenpark" ("Rules for the Human Zoo") in Elmau in Bavaria, during which he not only continued his perilous undertaking of bringing Heidegger back into the arena of legitimate thought, but also sketched a concomitant portrait of the liquidation of humanism. Yet even though doing so provoked considerable resistance and a major polemic (see chapter 4), Sloterdijk benefited from these incidents in terms of his reputation and national and international consecration as a major thinker. This cultural capital, acquired in the wake of his new status as a "European philosopher," enabled him to plunge into the intensive production of *Spheres*, the most ambitious works of his corpus.

Within the overall logic of his work, the Elmau talk is thematically consistent with a line of thinking begun in the 1990s with a series of philosophical and political texts and talks intended to draw out the *sites* of production of humanity. These writings were also part of an early-stage examination of issues that fueled the spherology project (see chapter 3), which, moreover, Sloterdijk wanted to promote during the storm engendered by the Elmau talk. Among these preparatory themes, the deconstruction of the abstract idea of the German nation,[4] the political reconsiderations entailed by the collapse of peace in the

Balkans,[5] and the enthusiasm for European development and its potential power,[6] not to mention the analysis of the notion of the people as a simple psycho-acoustic effect,[7] constitute a unified discourse that investigates the specific sites of human transmission, belonging, and culture.

As such, while "Rules for the Human Zoo" pursues the examination of this theme, it also radicalizes it to the point of provocation. In a disturbing manner, Sloterdijk expresses a few thoughts about the present and future state of the (post)humanist educational project through an examination of the means for the domestication of human beings by human beings. The argument has three components: (1) change of media – the crisis of literature and the end of the humanist educational project; (2) with Heidegger – rethinking humans in the world; and (3) against Heidegger – recovering anthropology and the duty of selection.

Change of media

Humanism is the domestication of humans through belles lettres. At the height of its art, humanism participates in the construction of citizenship by initiating youth into the canons of literature. The humanist project equally affects the edification of a national culture and sentimental education, in that this literature serves as a technics of domestication. It is said to inhibit savage impulses and brings young minds into contact with the best examples of sophisticated mores and language. In this light, Sloterdijk suggests that humanist literature consists in sending "thick letters to friends" (RHZ 12). These young addressees domesticate themselves through contact with these "letters," carefully selected by the state with a view to carrying out its cultivating mission and its own reproduction.

In Sloterdijk's view, a radical change occurred after 1945 in the order of literary mediation and self-domestication. Since the primacy of written media was replaced by that of mass media (radio and television), this overthrow – accelerated by network revolutions – has had adverse consequences. Whereas the age of classical humanism promoted self-domestication through the canons of belletristic literature, the arrival of the techno-media age engendered a reversal in the order of media that are supposed to fulfill the highest cultural functions:

> [M]odern societies can produce their political and cultural synthesis only marginally through literary, letter-writing, humanistic media. Of course, that does not mean that literature has come to an end, but it has split itself off and become a sui generis subculture, and the days of its value as bearer of the national spirit have passed. The social synthesis is no longer – and is no longer seen to be – primarily a matter of books and

letters. New means of political-cultural telecommunication have come
into prominence, which have restricted the pattern of script-born friendship to a limited number of people. The period when modern humanism
was the model for schooling and education has passed, because it is
no longer possible to retain the illusion that political and economic
structures could be organized on the amiable model of literary societies.
(RHZ 14)

The collapse of literary humanism is astonishing in light of the problem
of humanization. While humanists had for quite some time been able
to distinguish between inhibiting power (good readings) and disinhib-
iting power (the barbarism of entertainment), we are now faced with
distinguishing "between bestializing and taming tendencies" (RHZ
15). Such is the scope of the problem facing us: how to have humans
emerge from humans.

With Heidegger: world and technics

Sloterdijk keeps Heidegger's ideas close at hand in his thinking about
the emergence of human beings. Several elements favor this alliance
within the framework of the history of ideas. Like Sloterdijk, Heidegger
rejects Descartes and his vision based on the individual, doubt, and
general suspicion (see chapter 1). Both also elaborate their own version
of Romantic belonging in opposition to humanism, rational autonomy,
and the idea of a self-constructed subject. Shortly after World War II,
in his 1946 "Letter on Humanism,"[8] Heidegger had already developed
a bleak review of the militant humanisms (Bolshevism, Americanism,
and fascism) that had led to the destruction of humanity. In his view,
the excess of anthropocentrism common to these three modalities of
humanist violence stems from the belief in the infinite malleability of
the human animal, which calls for the right "breeding." Heidegger's
complaints are manifold. In his opposition to a *vitalist* or *naturalist*
reduction of what is at stake in the emergence of human beings, he
argues for an *existential* ontology that presents human beings in a
higher, more dignified manner. In his view, this dignity entails breaking
with the Enlightenment and shifting the focus from *human beings alone*
(the fiction of individual autonomy) to reveal their constitutive *non-
natural site* (the original source of belonging). To this end, Heidegger
introduces a new vocabulary. This novel ontology reworks the fundamental categories of existence so that they break with the Enlightenment. The self or the individual becomes *Dasein* (literally *Being-there*).
Heidegger uses this term both to designate human beings and to break
with the constitutive vocabulary of rationalist autonomy. Dasein is a
spatial creature or a being defined as having a fundamental relationship with its surroundings. Dasein's initial habitat is neither nature nor

what we now call the environment. So just *where* is it? Dasein's initial space is what Heidegger refers to as the *clearing*. This concept is crucial to Sloterdijk's global project, the outcome of which is spherology (see chapter 3). For the moment, it is important to keep in mind that the clearing is a metaphor that lies at the heart of Heidegger's ontological vision: Dasein can be found where there is a break in the opacity of nature, where a patch of sky opens up, making it possible to look up, and where there is enough light for Dasein to note its own existence. This fortuitous opening reveals that human beings are the product of a favorable space, like a breach seized upon in the general inhospitality of nature. A space of this kind able to generate humans is already unnatural. It is already a human world.

Sloterdijk takes up and comments on Heidegger's undertaking:

> At the heart of this antivitalistic passion lay the recognition that man is differentiated from animals in ontology, not in species or genus, so he cannot under any circumstances be considered an animal with a cultural or metaphysical addition. On the contrary: the form of being of the human itself is different from all vegetable and animal beings, because man has a world and is in the world, while plants and animals inhabit only a transitory environment. (RHZ 18)

This spatial motif, "from the clearing to the human-made world," is one of the distinctive features of Heidegger's thought that Sloterdijk intends to resuscitate in his own definition of human beings. This move is not a simple continuation, however. Nor is it exempt from polemic. What Sloterdijk takes from Heidegger is meant to support his own critique of humanism. With Heidegger's help, he discredits those who have forgotten that humans are above all beings-in-the-world. Because of this oversight, humanists cannot fulfill what they thought was their domesticating role. To this end, Sloterdijk thinks *with* Heidegger and uses the clearing notion to rethink the domestication task. However, Sloterdijk also finds himself thinking *against* Heidegger. In his inquiry into the spatiality of human self-engendering, he borrows elements from the heretical vocabularies of anthropology, paleontology, and biology. Sloterdijk is looking to enhance Heideggerian terminology with a bit of empirical grounding, even though the Black Forest Master so obstinately maintained his crypto-Catholic stance (RHZ 19), in which ontology occludes anthropology. It was because of this issue that Sloterdijk ultimately took a separate path.

Against Heidegger: anthropology and selection

In Sloterdijk's view, the exit from nature by human beings is the subject matter of the social history of the domestication of humans by humans and, as such, warrants closer examination. The hominization adventure primarily illustrates that this viviparous mammal systematically gives birth to premature creatures. This phenomenon already indicates that human beings emerge "with an ever-increasing excess of animalian unpreparedness" that already transforms "the transformation of bio-logical birth into the act of coming into the world" (RHZ 20). Heidegger had nevertheless kept this vocabulary of the anthropological revolu-tion at a distance: "Because of his obstinate suspicion of anthropology, and in his desire to maintain the ontological purity of the beginning of Dasein and being-in-the-world, Heidegger did not take sufficient account of this explosion" (RHZ 20). Yet, as Sloterdijk argues, above and beyond the bucolic clearing metaphor, human becoming in the world is also the bearer of a much more delicate history than ontologi-cal meditation would have us believe. In addition to drawing on an anthropological vocabulary, Sloterdijk's shift away from Heidegger is even more accentuated when he views the clearing as always having been prey to a politics of domestication. Despite the fact that Heidegger wants to break with militant humanisms, Sloterdijk believes, on the contrary, that the issue has always been and will always be unavoid-able in human history. We will always be faced with a heavy task – perilous and filled with taboos – that transforms the clearing into "a battleground and a place of decision and choice" (RHZ 21). This warrior vocabulary claimed by Sloterdijk raises some painful issues that can no longer be dealt with by the naivety of literary humanism. It is by invok-ing Nietzsche that he goes beyond Heidegger to introduce the issue of will in the art of domestication and engenderment. Sloterdijk intends to explore this dimension head on in a language and a vocabulary that exceed both humanism and the mystical, contemplative mantra of being-in-the-world.

The reflection undertaken in "Rules for the Human Zoo" becomes clearer in its political tones as Sloterdijk the anthropotechnologist coldly imagines the need for a new ruler in the human animal theme park. That domestication is a battleground in which competing visions confront one another is already clear for Nietzsche. Through the voice of his Zarathustra, Nietzsche views "man as a taming and nurturing power," and, more specifically, according to Sloterdijk, he claims that "modern men are primarily profitable breeders who have made out of wild men the Last Men" (RHZ 22).

Sloterdijk develops his interpretation on the basis of the following passages pasted together from *Thus Spoke Zarathustra*:

> For he [Zarathustra] wanted to learn what had transpired in the mean-time among human beings; whether they had become bigger or smaller. And once he saw a row of new houses, and he was truly amazed, and he said: "What do these houses mean? Truly, no great soul has placed them here, as a parable of itself!"

And these parlors and chambers, can *men* go in and out here?'

And Zarathustra stood still and reflected. At last he said sadly, "Everything has become smaller!"

Everywhere I see lower gateways; whoever is like me can still pass through, but – he has to stoop!

I walk among these people and keep my eyes open; they have become *smaller* and are becoming even smaller: *but this is because of their teaching on happiness and virtue.*

A few of them will, but most of them are merely willed.

Round, righteous and kind they are to one another, like grains of sand are round, righteous and kind to one another.

To modestly embrace a small happiness – that they call "resignation."

At bottom these simple ones want one simple thing: that no one harm them.

To them virtue is whatever makes modest and tame; this is how they made the wolf into the dog and mankind himself into mankind's favorite pet.[9]

This declaration discloses a will to domestication that Nietzsche views in a darker light than is the case for humanist optimism. Sloterdijk argues that Nietzsche "perceived a space in which the unavoidable battle over the direction of man-breeding would begin . . . He wants to . . . initiate a modern, momentous public battle between different breeders and breeding programs" (RHZ 22).

What is at stake in this competition? As we will discover in the third section of the present chapter, Sloterdijk adopts Nietzsche's perspective by opposing the horizontal trends of democratic equality to the vertical trends of heroic surpassing, that is, "those who wish to breed for minimization and those who wish to breed for maximization of human function" (RHZ 22).

For the moment, the incendiary, proto-fascist aspect of this kind of declaration (or its malevolent usage) is immediately tempered by a reference to classical literature in which this problem was viewed cold-bloodedly. Two and a half millennia before Nietzsche, Plato "presented his doctrine of the art of statesmanship entirely in pictures of shepherds and herds" (RHZ 26). This is a form of anthropotechnics that discloses itself again through metaphor:

The Platonic master finds the reason for his mastery only in the expertise he has in the odd and peculiar art of breeding. Here we see the

reemergence of the expert-king, whose justification is the insight about
how, without doing damage to their free will, human beings can best sort
themselves out and make connections. Royal anthropotechnology, in
short, demands of the statesman that he understand how to bring
together free but suggestible people in order to bring out the characteristics that are most advantageous to the whole, so that under his direction
the human zoo can achieve the optimum homeostasis. (RHZ 26)

A statesperson is an artisan who weaves the fabric that holds the city
together. Although Sloterdijk's might seem to be a curious choice of
metaphor, it is consistent with his general observation concerning
breeding programs. There are plenty of "discourses which speak of
human society as if it were a zoo which is at the same time a theme
park: the keeping of men in parks or stadiums seems from now on a
zoo-political task. What are presented as reflections on politics are actu-
ally foundational reflections on rules for the maintenance of the human
zoo" (RHZ 25). The goal of this description of the art of politics is to
draw out the issue of the breeding of human beings – these "self-
fencing, self-shepherding creatures" (RHZ 25) – much more directly
than the old literary humanism currently being steamrollered by media
networks and biogenetic manipulations:

> The domestication of man is the great unthinkable, from which human-
> ism from antiquity to the present has averted its eyes. Recognizing this
> suffices to plunge us into deep waters . . . It is characteristic of our tech-
> nological and anthropotechnological age that people willingly fall more
> and more into the active, or agent, side of selection, without having to
> be forced into the role of selectors. As evidence, it can be noted that
> there is something suspicious in the power of the vote, and it will soon
> become one way of avoiding guilt for people to explicitly refuse to exer-
> cise the power of selection that they actually have available to them.
> (RHZ 23–4)

While the Elmau talk took the form of a commentary on "Letter on
Humanism," as a stepping-stone for a reflection on the contemporary
state of affairs, Sloterdijk's diagnosis could hardly be described as
music to democratic ears. Both humanism and breeding through belletristic literature have disappeared. This void brings the issue of
domestication to the fore. Since humans have failed in their "animality," the problem of their breeding will always be present. As such,
selection is this unthought-of aspect that has resurfaced, though in an
imprecise and hesitant manner. The reason for this is that the heirs of
humanism and the Enlightenment are unable to walk in these shoes, a
failing that Sloterdijk views as a real problem. Indeed, we cannot continually refuse to grasp the scope of this problem, since "[it] is characteristic of being human that human beings are presented with tasks

that are too difficult for them, without having the option of avoiding them because of their difficulty" (RHZ 24).

Romancing the Stone: World as Lithotechnics

The pan-European polemic engendered by the Elmau talk clouded the skies over the unavoidable, overly intense discussion of this issue. This dispute, which saw Sloterdijk facing off with Habermas, is covered in chapter 4 and must be treated separately, since it is the meta-level of this controversy (the place occupied by Heidegger and Nietzsche within legitimate thought) that played a preponderant and decisive role in earning greater renown for Sloterdijk. However, to do justice to the undertaking, which is only partly sketched in this first reflection on the clearing and on the domestication of human beings, it is important here to follow Sloterdijk a bit further in the rearticulation of Heidegger as a theorist of technics.

In *Nicht gerettet* (*Not Saved*), a collection of essays providing a wider view of his posthumanist arguments, Sloterdijk develops his sense of anthropotechnics. In the collection's centerpiece, "Domestikation des Seins" ("Domestication of Being"), he appropriates the Heideggerian couplet of clearing–world, but does so with a view to extracting it from its mystical or contemplative use and grounding it in the concreteness of anthropology and the hominization process. To characterize his sense of the clearing, Sloterdijk forges another of his famous reversible terms with two meanings. He writes about "onto-anthropology" – at the crossroads of Heidegger's *onto*logical intuitions and Dieter Claessens's *anthro*pological work – and it is only via this approach that the problems overlooked by humanism can be addressed:

> The expulsion from the routines of humanism is the major logical event of the period which cannot be avoided by hiding behind good will . . . In the field of the history of the mind and technics, the most striking characteristic of the world situation is precisely the fact that technoculture has produced a new aggregate state of language and texts that has practically nothing more to do with their traditional interpretations by religion, metaphysics and humanism. (NG 212)

This technoculture or anthropotechnics is the new area of research that must be tackled by contemporary theory. This task must rid itself of humanist thought because, rather than isolating humanity, it must be thought of in terms of its intimate relationship with technics. In contrast to a humanism that chooses the primacy of the subject (human beings) over the disturbing object (technics), this task comes back to what is explicit in Heidegger: the coextensiveness and co-creation of humans and the clearing, which is to say the hybridity of human beings and technics. To fully grasp this line of argument, it should be noted that Sloterdijk discredits all dichotomy-based approaches to this problem. He critiques this "anti-technological hysteria," which is "reactionary in the essential sense of the word, because it expresses the ressentiment of those who cling to outdated dichotomies and reject complexities they fail to understand" (NG 223).[10] This "failure to understand" is the inability to think about human beings as products of the autogenous world or anthropotechnics complex that constitutes them:

> In contrast to this religiously-flavoured battle surrounding human beings, the anthropotechnical expression takes shape within the framework of efforts towards a clear theory of historical anthropology according to which humans themselves are fundamentally products and can only be understood if we focus on their conditions of production . . . the human condition is entirely a product and a result – but a product of manufacturing rarely seen before and adequately described as such and a result of processes, the conditions and rules of which are still poorly understood. (NG 152–3)

Although the formulas derived from anthropotechnics still remain somewhat abstract and polemical, Sloterdijk has arrived at a point at which his fantastical narrative has attained its most concrete level. It is here that disclosure via myth reveals the paths to overcoming the nature/culture divide. Briefly stated, Sloterdijk's onto-anthropology dares to put the clearing *and* technics at the same level, to the point of transgressing Heidegger's thought. The "house of being" is no longer language, but the tool. In the beginning was not the word, but stone.

According to Sloterdijk,[11] the first manifestations of lithotechnics gave a very material sense to the notion of the clearing: "The prehuman produces the first holes and cracks into the environment fence when he, by means of throws and blows, becomes the author of a distance technique, that has repercussions on himself " (NG 180).[12] Three terms are highly charged here: *cracks*, *throws*, and *blows*. Regarding *cracks*, humans and stones break apart the natural given. This initially modest breach or clearing will never close again and will constitute their habitat, or, in other words, their immunological reaction to their self-expulsion from nature. As for *throws*, the throwing of a stone is the first concrete delimitation of the clearing's territory: the stone thrown by a human hand circumscribes a field of action, sets in motion the first calculations of causes and effects, and is the first school of theory. For their part, *blows* signify that the stone is also a weapon: "the human animal drives every unwanted being out of his 'living space' and produces a protected space."[13] This spirit of vigilance in this space banished from nature is coextensive with human beings. It grows to the same extent as the sophistication of the stone and the hand that holds it. As suggested by the cinematographic fable *2001: A Space Odyssey*, the primitive throwing of a stone is the great anthropotechnic leap that is only a few small throws away from the orbital space station.

Four anthropotechnic mechanisms

Disclosure, *aletheia* (revealing), and *apokalupsis* (uncovering): technics *reveals* the truth about human beings. It *uncovers* and explicitly discloses what shapes and conditions them. There is no longer any subject–object bivalence. Technics is the "point of departure and of arrival"[14] because humans and technics arise from common ancestors:

> *Nous sommes sur un plan où il y a principalement de la technique.*[15] If we are able to say "there are" human beings, it is because technology made them emerge out of pre-humanity. It is precisely that which yields humans or the basis upon which "there can be human beings." Afterwards, nothing strange will happen to human beings when they expose themselves to a new product or process, and they will do nothing perverse when they mutate via auto-technics to the extent that these interventions and aids occur at the level of understanding the biological and social "nature" of human beings and that genuine, intelligent and productive co-productions with a development potential can be efficacious. (NG 225)

Sloterdijk quickly nuances what could be confused with a kind of naive technophilia here. For the moment, it is important to retain the fact that the three keywords of lithotechnics (*cracks*, *throws*, and *blows*) are unified under a fourth word: *distance*. On the basis of this very concrete image of the stone that is thrown – the inaugural moment of culture and/or last "event" in human natural history – Sloterdijk returns to the path of his anthropodicy. With the help of a few selected texts from anthropological studies of the 1920s, he decomposes anthropogenesis into four mechanisms of distance-taking from "Mother Nature" (see NG 175–211).

The first mechanism is *insulation*. The life of gregarious animals creates the specific, fragile climatic conditions that insulate offspring from the immediate pressures of nature. In so doing, the criteria of evolution are not dictated by the environment, but circumvented or supported by the unprecedented space that this group generates via a wall, composed of their living bodies, that sees to the protection of a gentler interiority. In this regard, the mother–child incubator, as insulation within insulation, is the carrier of the most important consequence of the first mechanism, that of prolonging childhood and opening a field of evolutionary experimentation beyond nature's grip.

The second mechanism is activated by the exponential consequences of the first rudimentary uses of stone by human beings. Lithotechnics, followed by the generalization of tool use, does not increase the brute strength of the body that it suppresses or replaces with a machine. This second mechanism thus designates this _disconnection or deactivation of the body_ that not only breaks with surrounding nature,[16] but also distances the body from its action, now freed from the physical limits of human muscles.

Once lightened by technics, the body becomes more refined and displays increasingly sophisticated and luxurious features. Since it lives in this clearing insulated from the pressures of natural selection, this body foils evolutionism by "using the climate and exploiting possibilities in a setting that tends to reward aesthetic variations" (NG 187–8). This third mechanism concerns this aesthetic power acquired by human bodies within the openness of the clearing. In line with earlier work,[17] Sloterdijk denotes this autoplastic power with the terms _neoteny_ and _paedomorphis_, that is, the conservation of fetal traits, and prolonging childhood into adulthood. The fact that the birth of human offspring is systematically premature – because of the handicap of having an especially large cerebral cortex – provides the evolutionary occasion to prolong the protective capacity of the womb by adult groupings. The cunning of technics is such that this risky, premature biological state becomes stable, and engenders an aesthetic trend that refines the delicacy of hairless faces and softened hands capable of sophisticated prehension and exercises. This exaggeration in prolonging fetal attributes and in delaying adult characteristics is nothing more than a luxurious aspect lying at the heart of anthropotechnics. The ascending curve of human beauty is the result of a very long history. It is a refinement that is also co-constitutive of the species inasmuch as infancy and luxury have become synonyms of care:

> Because the bodies of pre-humans have increasingly become gilded bodies – and all luxury begins by being able to be immature, to maintain and live to the limit a childhood past, – human beings must take good care of themselves and become attentive animals, living creatures that now take steps concerning the next day and the day after. (NG 193)

The fourth mechanism – _transference_ (_Übertragung_) – emerges from the earliest stage of the clearing, its gradual establishment as an externalized womb, and its refinements to the physical and cultural characteristics of the species. This transference mechanism is the capacity of human groupings to equip themselves with cultural and symbolic prostheses that both protect and emulate the fragile space of their hyper-insulation: for example, language, religious rituals, and houses. Prostheses of this kind _protect_ because this type of open, luxurious space can always be destroyed from the outside. This fragility requires that a cultural routine be adopted, one that makes it possible to incorporate a high degree of vigilance and foresight. Prostheses of this kind *emulate* because whenever this type of space is destroyed, the exiled must "be able to restore former states of integrity (even in the event of wounds and collapse) and to draw on a reservoir of memories and routines making it possible to replicate former states of integrity" (NG 208).

Transference is the regenerative capacity of lost immunity. It is a key notion in spherology (see chapter 3) and its inquiry into habitation modes as the first clearing's sophisticated prostheses. Although the notion of transference belongs to the vocabulary of psychoanalysis, Sloterdijk rejects its pessimism. Childhood's ecstatic states are not lost forever.

Allo- and homeo-technics

"History began earlier than those who have recounted it believe" (NG 193). Sloterdijk's narrative about the major mechanisms of anthropotechnics is certainly appealing. For the reader of philosophy who is somewhat of a neophyte with regard to anthropology, this *poiesis* of species has the merit of showing that the emergence of human beings is a much older matter than, say, the Aristotelian mastery of Logos. To demonstrate this claim, Sloterdijk takes theories here and there from sciences (anthropology and paleontology) neglected by philosophers, to compensate for the gaps in their time-schemes and to align them with the long history of the origin of human culture. The seductiveness of Sloterdijk's narrative is also due to the considerable clarity and the elimination of false dichotomies in its approach to highly complex issues. The soothing effect of this tale consists precisely in exploiting the depths of these bivalences to enable readers to shed the convenient habits of technophobic thought, which is blind, if not delusional, with regard to the technical nature of *Homo sapiens*. In light of this very long history, the hypocritical alarmism of several moralists about the dangers of biotechnologies is surely disarmed: are not the finest cheeses and alcoholic beverages respectively the result of mycological bacteriological processes? Are they not examples of biotechnologies much older than the Bronze Age?[18]

However, the soothing state Sloterdijk seeks to bring about does not give rise to conventional technophilia, which, alongside a sci-fi imagination, would entail outflanking technophobia by advocating for the control of the undesirable human factor by recourse to errorless machines. It is precisely this hierarchical game that Sloterdijk attacks by arguing instead in favor of homeotechnics, which offers the only tools compatible with sustainable anthropotechnics.

Metaphorically following Hahnemann's homeopathic axiom of *similia similibus curantur* ("like is cured by like"), homeotechnics is a formula that suggests that humans and technics are partners in their mutual health: "Homeotechnics is more like cooperation than domination . . . The major circumstances of homeotechnics are critical cases of co-intelligence" (NG 228).

In this kind of co-institutive relation, there is neither master nor slave. To come back to the disturbing images that are part of the fantastical style that Sloterdijk adopts in this onto-anthropology, we are at a level at which there are only monstrosity and hybridity. All that enters the clearing defined by anthropotechnic space is irreversibly deviated from its natural course and drawn into the orbit of the plastic power of human beings. This domesticating clearing, like that of our overly domesticated, overly protected animal pets, is a permanent field of biotechnical experimentation, a culture of monstrous luxury.

Homeo- and allo-technique present two opposing visions of technics: the first accompanies and protects human beings; the second oppresses and annihilates them. Within the framework of true *homeotechnics*, there is no foreseeable gain possible to the detriment of a partner. As such, it moves beyond heteronomy, the postulate of the necessary domination of one partner by the other that was always characteristic of humanist thought. When applied to technics, heteronomy becomes *allotechnics*, a perversion of anthropotechnics, "the major circumstances [of which] are always those in which the struggles for preferential access by means of rape and destruction occur" (NG 227). Allotechnics is the fruit of modern humanism, which has remained a prisoner of the nefarious dichotomies of traditional metaphysics. It inserts a bivalence between subject and object, master and slave, or friend and foe, and when it takes the form of the authority of the state traversed by suspicion and paranoia, it attains an unequaled destructive potential. This destruction by technology rises up as a barrier to the calming effect of homeotechnics:

> The assumption that the suspicious mood will remain the realistic one in the future is most strongly confirmed by the actions of US strategists, who in August of 1945 did not refrain from employing the most extreme allotechnological weapon, the atom bomb, directly against humans. In doing this, they provided an epochal argument for the suspicion against the alliance between the highest technology and the most lowly subjectivity. Due to Hiroshima, humans have reason to believe that the most advanced technologies are uninhibited and reason to distrust the Oppenheimers and Trumans of genetics. (NG 229–30)[19]

This somewhat sobering note evokes a partial list, to say the least, of the allotechnic crimes that have marked the twentieth century. Nevertheless, it serves as a realistic word of warning against the therapeutic program prescribed by Sloterdijk: whosoever wants to be healed of allotechnics must overcome the modern death drive and choose life.

Out of the Clearing and into the Gym: The Anthropotechnics of Self-improvement

With the publication of *You Must Change Your Life* and *The Art of Philosophy*, Sloterdijk came back to his anthropotechnics project, following a 10-year hiatus during which he completed the *Spheres* trilogy and contributed to the study of post-9/11 mentalities (see TA, RT, and TPWP). However, this return to arguments formulated at the turn of the millennium adopted a new tone and new concerns. Firstly, Sloterdijk no longer situated himself on the field of polemics that had smothered the calm reception of his program aimed at managing the domestication of humans by humans.[20] Secondly, he discarded the "We" of the species elements of his technological, anthropological, and paleontological vocabulary in favor of focusing exclusively on a "You" imperative aimed at self-improvement through exercise. This later anthropotechnics is less about space-centered creatures than about self-created exercisers. The exaggeration of the openness of the clearing became the exaggeration "of orthodox retreats to the practising and artistically heightened life" (MCL 298).

Anthropotechnics is redefined as *practice*, consisting of "methods of mental and physical practising by which humans from the most diverse cultures have attempted to optimize their cosmic and immunological status in the vague risks of living and acute certainties of death" (MCL 10). It is important to note this shift in meaning. Although Sloterdijk begins by taking up the metaphor of symbolic prosthetics that must support the immunology of human cultures, it is no longer in the collective sense of the species or of equality. Rather, it is in the sense of exceptional individuals who feel the call of "vertical tension." This will is that of the possessive pronoun: "In my most conscious moment, I am affected by the absolute objection to my status quo: my change is the one thing that is necessary. If you do indeed subsequently change your life, what you are doing is no different from what you desire with your whole will as soon as you feel how a vertical tension that is valid for you unhinges your life" (MCL 26). Symbolic immunological practice stands apart from stones or from mothers and becomes a will to transcendence, to "becoming more" (MCL 176) and to resisting mediocrity:

> The hero of the following account, *Homo immunologicus*, who must give his life, with all its dangers and surfeits, a symbolic framework, is the

human being that struggles with itself in concern for its form. We will
characterize it more closely as the ethical human being, or rather *Homo
repetitivus*, *Homo artista*, the human in training. (MCL 10)

Sloterdijk claims that this life of practicing has not received its fair share
of attention by philosophers. This neglect is due to the fact that in
antiquity, there was a distinction between the *vita contemplativa* and the
vita activa, and moderns have eyes only for production and labor. Yet
the life of practicing corresponds neither to the ancient categorization
nor to the invasion of productive activity: "By nature, this is a mixed
domain: it seems contemplative without relinquishing characteristics
of activity and active without losing the contemplative perspective"
(AP 6). Nor is it production, since it has no influence on external objects.
On the contrary, it is self-referential and concerns only those who exercise and develop their "state of capability" (AP 6). Sloterdijk's emphasis
on the power of practicing appears to downgrade technology or
worldly space in the search for the fundamental categories of self-
taming. These two elements, which had been very present in the first
formulation of the anthropotechnic hypothesis, are now relegated
instead to the domain of spherology (chapter 3). It is now a matter of
considering self-taming by way of the many faces of practicing: athlete,
acrobat, virtuoso, ascetic, monk, coach, guru, professor, writer, Bud-
dhist master, impersonator of Christ.[21]

This difference in emphasis, fueled by a voluble enthusiasm for the
virtues of exercise, even manages to make practicing the true means of
transcending the nature/culture divide. The technical essence of human
beings is above all voluntary: "In truth, the crossing from nature to
culture and vice versa has always stood wide open. It leads across an
easily accessible bridge: the practising life" (MCL 11). This bridge built
on accumulated practicing is not a means for reconciling opposites. It
is a means for leaving an inferior shore to reach a superior one and, as
such, is related more to a "disposable ladder" (MCL 178). Indeed, later
anthropotechnics is situated within a wealth of oppositions between
high and low, virtuosity and equality, or verticality and horizontality,
the overcoming of which entails dismissing one of the parts.[22] Bivalence
and dichotomy thus find their way back into the core of Sloterdijk's
concerns and prescriptions, though not to proliferate double meanings
and circumvent the principle of non-contradiction, but to conclude the
anthropotechnic tale with a unilateral ending. At the least, the presentation by oppositions and hierarchizations enables us to accurately recon-
stitute the prevailing mood in the gymnasium of the athletes of virtue.
We will thus follow the discourse of our sports commentator as he
describes this bestiary of ascetic performances in line with best or worst
practice, and as he hierarchizes them as a function of a ranking that
rates them by Nietzschean and Foucauldian score cards, respectively.

Good and bad ascesis

Throughout his work, Sloterdijk never shies away from the systematic use of Nietzsche as precursor, forerunner, model, or guide. Anthropotechnics is no exception to this rule. Taking up the passage in *Zarathustra* regarding the critique of common virtues and the last human beings who no longer want for anything, Sloterdijk turns his attention to the problem of desiring to be something – of wanting "the authority of a different life in this life" (MCL 25–6). However, as much as Nietzsche is an ally, Sloterdijk must dissociate himself from the outset from Nietzsche's overly quick condemnation of the ascetic ideal, so as to draw out the meaning of good and bad ascesis.

This effort to shift the Nietzschean critique as it was formulated in *On the Genealogy of Morality* begins with the acknowledgment that ascesis has a bad side.[23] An ill-conceived, bilious, and vindictive ascesis served as a vehicle for ressentiment, the "vengeful attitude . . . born of disclaimed envy, rebellious inferiority, and the deferred need for revenge of a caste of power-crazy clerics and agitators" (AP 37). This ascesis or asceticism of the sick and of priests is pathological and at war with life. It is bad ascesis.

Sloterdijk wants instead to bring about a "rebirth of antiquity," namely "a regression to a time in which the changing of life had not yet fallen under the command of life-denying asceticisms" (MCL 36); that is, "a revitalization of the motifs of the practising life" (MCL 212). In this regard, Nietzsche's status as a precursor was reaffirmed because he was the very first to have viewed antiquity as an ascetic planet "inhabited by the practising, the aspiring and the virtuosos" (MCL 35).[24] This positive ascesis, which Sloterdijk wishes with all his heart to call upon as the cornerstone of a general ascetology, is that of prodigies who "impose their regulations on themselves because they see them as a means of reaching their optimum as thinkers and creators of works" (MCL 36).

At a time when Europe appeared to be heading toward democracy, material comfort, and egalitarianism, Nietzsche was "the only one who unconditionally embraced the primacy of the vertical" (MCL 177). The good Nietzsche and the good ascesis are part and parcel of good anthropotechnics:

> Nietzsche's occasional misinterpretation cannot detract from the value of his discovery. With his find, Nietzsche stands fatally – in the best sense of the word – at the start of modern, non-spiritualistic ascetologies along with their physio- and psychotechnic annexes, with dietologies and self-referential trainings, and hence all the form of self-referential practising and working on one's own vital form that I bring together in the term "anthropotechnics." (MCL 34)

The term thus received a new meaning. Whether it is impoverished or enriched is a matter of interpretation. What is certain is that it is now entwined with the will to change their life displayed by those who practice. The clearing is to natural space what exercise is to the eternal return of the same: "Only in this framework can one call upon humans to cross over from the even years of being into the dramatic situation of a project time" (MCL 243). Such is the terrain of good ascesis.

Good and bad exercises

While Nietzsche is the inventor of ascetology, Foucault is acknowledged as the discipline's best athlete. In his revised and corrected anthropotechnics, Sloterdijk has nothing but praise for the "early and late Foucault" (MCL 177), whom he associates with a heroic penchant that does not settle for life in base camps. This Foucault is the one who confirmed the fecundity of "the history of modern disciplinary procedures" (MCL 323) and, as such, warranted inclusion among Sloterdijk's greatest sources of inspiration.[25] This return to basics takes place within a framework of homage and debt, in that Sloterdijk sees in the right Foucault the ultimate theorist of "General Disciplinics" (MCL 155), which is made up of at least 13 elements:

> (1) acrobatics and aesthetics including the system of art forms and genres . . . (2) athletics (the general study of sporting forms) to (3) rhetoric or sophistry, then (4) therapeutics in all its specialized branches, (5) epistemics (including philosophy), (6) a general study of professions (including the 'applied arts', which are assigned to the field of *arts et métiers* and (7) the study of machinistic technologies. It also includes (8) administrativics . . . (9) the encyclopaedia of meditation systems . . . (10) ritualistics . . . (11) the study of sexual practices, (12) gastronomics and finally (13) the open list of cultivatable activities, whose openness means the interminability of the discipline-forming and thus the subjectification-enabling field itself. (MCL 156–7)

Sloterdijk claims that Foucault himself had touched upon seven of these elements, "which tells us enough about Foucault's panathletic qualities" (MCL 157). But just how do Foucauldian heroism and rehabilitation of the vast terrain of disciplinics inform us about good and bad exercises? From Foucault, one must take the optimistic attitude that rose above the harsh, ressentiment-laden critique of power: "I do not want to destroy anything."[26] For their part, we can recognize good exercises whenever they take the form of catapults, as we shall go on to see.

Good exercises are forms of ascension: verticality, rupture with base camps, separation from the ordinary, living differently in this life, and getting to the other side. It is for this reason that "cultural theory can only be meaningfully carried out as the description of catapults" (MCL 190). This principle of projecting oneself beyond the inertia of routine is not for everyone – *a few of them will, but most of them are merely willed* – because it is an exemplary feature of the elite: "They are the provocateurs of the future, who build the catapults for shots into the supraordinary" (MCL 192). Good exercises are accomplished in small groups that pull back. This withdrawal is itself the first condition of erectile exercises. To erect ethical models, "spaces for retreat for elites" (MCL 272) are needed. No advanced civilization can see the light of day without the contribution of these "secessionarily [*sic*] isolated groups ... whose general form appears in an ethics of stabilized improbability" (MCL 272). Good exercises are rare, exceptional, and foundational elements of culture:

> The remoulding of humans as carriers of explicit practice programmes in the more advanced civilizations not only leads to the eccentric self-relation of existence in spiritual enclaves. It also imposes a radically altered sense of time and the future on the practising. In reality, the adventure of advanced civilizations consists in lifting an existential time out of the cosmic, universally shared time. (MCL 243)

Let us examine this description of good exercises in light of the rapprochement of Nietzsche and Foucault proposed by Sloterdijk. If *elite* and *high civilization* are mantras uttered by a Nietzsche who was worried by the democratic platitudes and miserable socialism against which he furiously raged in his correspondence throughout the 1870s, one may wonder whether Foucault's care of the self stems from the same concerns. Perhaps there is more of a difference in context here than in approach and perspective.

In his 1984 Collège de France lectures, Foucault dwells less on the elite or their civilized sophistication than on Diogenes of Sinope, one of their spiteful, scathing critics. The poverty and quite certainly athletic, ascetic performance of this illustrious representative of biting kynicisim (see chapter 1) was a stone in the shoes of the sophisticated elite who so wanted to break with the animal kingdom. By way of a bridge between their performances, we can note that the later Foucault was enthralled by what was the focal point for the early Sloterdijk, namely, the radical (if jovial) critique of civilization's schizophrenic dualisms. The later Foucault's reply, as he was exiting the stage, was to praise cynics and Diogenes – insolence and putting oneself at risk through parrhesia – whereas the later Sloterdijk no longer wears the mantle of his younger self. Another sign of this irony: the new anthropotechnics makes no explicit mention of Diogenes and becomes allusive whenever it talks about the virtuosos of biting wit. In fact, the aging Sloterdijk, who unabashedly reveals himself in *Zeilen und Tage*

(*Lines and Days*), is quite concerned with the comfort of airplanes and the decor of the hotels he has visited on the international circuit of a global scholar. These elements cohabit with cynical-kynical tidbits, in which Sloterdijk compares students to Ming vases, worries about general obesity, sings the beauty of women photographed without their knowledge, delights in learning about the details of Weber's masochistic sexual life, and cheerfully imagines seeing Hegel in front of a television.

Good and bad hierarchy

An elitist position must be able to maintain a rational discourse on the need for hierarchy. Sloterdijk does not avoid the matter and clarifies his position on many occasions by resorting to nuance or sarcasm with regard to egalitarian pathos. Although hierarchy is of a "binding nature" (MCL 12), it has nothing to do with domination, medieval nobility, or class society. Anthropotechnics seeks to show "how the shift from a theory of class society (with vertical differentiation through dominance, repression and privilege) to a theory of discipline society (with vertical differentiation through asceticism, virtuosity and achievement) can take place" (MCL 132). It is thus a merit-based hierarchy, a rejection of the idea of privilege-based superiority. In this regard, Sloterdijk molds himself to the revolutionary vocabulary used by Sieyès (abolition of privileges) while directing it away from its ends (equality of functions);[27] nor is it a matter of exploring the equality hypothesis cherished by Jacques Rancière.[28] So just what is the sense of good hierarchy?

Good hierarchy allows practices – necessarily from a minority – that overcome inertia and routine and that result in surprises that overly egalitarian sociologists would tend to overlook or occlude. By opposition to what it is not, we learn that good hierarchy is neither more nor less than a means of resisting barbarism. Barbarians are those "who [refuse] to acknowledge any ranking rules or hierarchy" (MCL 12). Anti-elitism amounts to confinement to base camps and increases the load borne by those wishing to go on an expedition to the summits. It is at this point that Sloterdijk attacks Bourdieu's concept of habitus. Even though he appreciates his "satire without laughs about the *nouveaux riches* and the ambitious" (MCL 181), it is the primacy of inertia implied by the concept of habitus (the social within one) that Sloterdijk critiques.[29] He does not think that human authenticity should be limited to class belonging, and claims that Bourdieu "cannot grasp the individualized forms of existential self-designs" (MCL 181).

Elected base-camp guardian, along with Habermas (whose deeply rooted universalism and moralizing ethic of public debate he had nevertheless frequently attacked), Bourdieu is, in Sloterdijk's view, the quintessential egalitarian sociologist who advocates a definitive installation on the plains at a remove from the summits. Though the accusation is impetuous, it serves only to bring to the forefront the good old foundational quarrels of sociology, which remains divided between individualism and holism. To be sure, Bourdieu is not only the author of *La distinction*. Taking his private life as raw material, he confesses – in a posthumously published work – that sociology talks to itself, adding "[h]ow could I fail to recognize myself in Nietzsche when he says, roughly, in *Ecce Homo*, that he has only ever attacked things that he knew well, that he had himself experienced, and that, up to a point, he had himself been?"[30] We are born determined and have but a very small chance of becoming free, said Bourdieu. This common lot serves as a basis for solidarity, which is not synonymous with egoistically individual rescue. The question remains, however, as to whether a sociology of oppression inhibits life improvement. Should it be listed among bad exercises? Bourdieu's final words soberly answered in the negative: "[N]othing would make me happier than having made it possible for some of my readers to recognize their own experiences, difficulties, questionings, sufferings, and so on, in mine, and to draw from that realistic identification, which is quite the opposite of an exalted projection, some means of doing what they do, and living what they live, a little bit better."[31]

Good and bad imperatives

"[D]emocracy . . . is not as such a valid reason to do away with all forms of vertical tension" (MCL 277). Equality and democracy are confinements in the base camps of the quest for human elevation. As such, they cannot be viewed as good imperatives, although they are not the worst evils that one can meet on the road to humanity's self-design.

The worst imperatives are not established in liberal societies or in field theory. Indeed, Sloterdijk notes that they were formulated and took shape in soviet communism. In drawing attention to the origin of the concept of anthropotechnics, Sloterdijk is obliged to dissociate himself from its inaugural formulation, which unfortunately took form in the 1920s in the Soviet Union.[32] In his view, this usage is of a dubious nature since it is governed by a bad maxim: species, serial, format, collective. In rejecting spiritual, vertical tension, this "biopolitical utopianism" (MCL 399) was interested only in the material base, in the technical, physical element, that is, the biological body rendered infinitely malleable. Soviet anthropotechnics "tears down the boundary between being and phantasm" (MCL 399), which permitted the culture of camps that "served repression on the pretext of re-education, extermination on the pretext of work, and finally eradication without pretext" (MCL 426).[33]

This anti-communist rage dotting the final pages of *You Must Change Your Life* acts as a kind of continental divide between the cure offered by the good anthropotechnic maxim and the poison of its counterfeits. The (re)introduction of a few dichotomies of this kind along his way leads one to believe that Sloterdijk has at last broken with the first formulation of anthropotechnics. The material (the stone) and the shared (the species) elements, as well as the autoplastic or fanciful element, are associated here with the soviet specter from which he absolutely wants to dissociate himself. In revaluing individualism (of the will) and spiritualism (of vertical exercising), he disturbs or radically redefines his starting observations about the co-constitution of human beings in the existential relationship with space and other. Indeed, it is not to the Soviets but to the poet Rainer Maria Rilke that he owes the title of and the inspiration for his last anthropotechnic work. Inspired by an antique sculpture of the torso of Apollo, Rilke experienced the call of verticality upon contact with this example of artistic perfection (MCL 21). This call is the key to the good anthropotechnic maxim addressed to individuals who impose the rules of living differently in this life: "[a]lways behave in such a way that the account of your development could serve as the schema of a generalizable history of completion!" (MCL 253).

This imperative is egoist and voluntary. It calls out to a "You" and affirms itself as an "I" in refusing the control of bad habits in favor of developing good ones. The egoism advocated here stems from an attitude akin to the morals of the philosopher Max Stirner and of Nietzsche: "egotism is often merely the despicable pseudonym of the best of human possibilities" (MCL 242). The good anthropotechnic maxim does not ask its subjects to choose between themselves and the world. On the contrary, it postulates that a better world can emerge only out of decisions favoring better exercises, out of individuals who want to put themselves to the test, and out of a willing conversion.

It is by touching the chord of the very common desire to change one's life – the rage and impulse that declare, with regard to our personal problems and the routines smothering us, "I wish to leave the continuum of the false and the harmful" (MCL 209) – that Sloterdijk becomes quite deft. He convincingly draws out what all democratic citizens promise to themselves every day or every year in those moments in which they have the honesty to admit to themselves that they are in the grip of routines that go against their most conscious and highest aspirations. Those who have already felt and responded to this call may vibrate now and then at the same frequency as Sloterdijk's argument for the role of heights and the upright stance. They need no jargon to know what it is to be able to count on self-reliance.

To amplify matters, Sloterdijk, who well knows that what he is saying ineluctably refers to himself – the marathon man of writing – ultimately makes self-reliance a reason for unbridled self-praise: "The imperative 'You must change your life!' . . . implies taking oneself in hand and moulding one's own existence into an object of admiration" (MCL 326). This megalomania that so exasperates the false humility of morality is in fact filled with therapeutic virtues that will be explored in chapter 5.

3

Spherology

"Spherology is the method by which it is possible to increase the spacious dimensions of the world several million fold whereas current globalization discourses reduce the world in a disgusting manner" (ZT 131). This chapter focuses on the spatial turn in Sloterdijk's work, which is devoted to developing spherology, a postphenomenological analysis of human spatiality. There is no clear distinction between the narrative proposed by anthropotechnics (chapter 2) and the one that unfolds within *Spheres*. Spherology also resonates with psychopolitics and its emphasis on the construction of a mental ambience. Still, if there is a need to treat them separately for the purposes of clarifying the work's approaches and thematic divisions, it must above all be kept in mind that the analyses in chapters 2 and 3 are in concord with one another and share a single focus, namely the notion of a *spatial species*. However, while anthropotechnics may have had a polemical dimension focused on discrediting the humanist tradition (anti-technological) and egalitarian (anti-elitist) sociologists, spherology has few if any such ambitions, since it serves, rather, as a positive perspective. Indeed, spherology proposes a therapeutic strategy that prescribes an alter-modernity or pharmakon that Sloterdijk grinds in his own mortar.

This spherological remedy involves a twofold prescription. Firstly, it praises the virtues of the kind of strong belonging that undermines the supremacy of hawkish, bourgeois subjectivity, which Sloterdijk refers to as *projecting into the Small*. Secondly, far from being blind to the macrological nature of our times, this therapeutic strategy must reconcile itself with modern monstrosity and rewrite the narrative of the unfolding of a hyper-complex society, the contemporary structure and coherence of which no longer respond to modernity's control schemes and self-fulfilling prophecies, which Sloterdijk refers to as *projecting into the Big*. This chapter will focus primarily on this second aspect of spherology and provide an account of this spatial theorization as a political phenomenon, which directly responds to the issue of the organization of coexistence by means of common tuning and co-immunity. The discussion will dwell more particularly on the macro-social dimension of spherology rather than on its intimate dimension (which will be specifically addressed in chapter 5), notwithstanding the fact that these moments are inseparable within the general economy of Sloterdijk's thought.

Spatial Turn

The *Spheres* cycle is a vast collection of cosmological and architectural traces that works toward an understanding and exhaustive description of the sites of production of human beings. From a philosophical perspective, spherology is intended as a contribution to Heidegger's existential phenomenology, reviewed and revised through the lens of an anthropology of the clearing (see chapter 2), transposed here into a spherical habitat. It is in this precise sense that spherology participates in a kind of *postphenomenology*, which, while it de-romanticizes Heidegger and makes him "one of the most important founders of the philosophy of technology,"[1] retains his concern for belonging and the definition of Dasein as both a creature and a creator of spaces. As such, this spatial pattern takes up Heidegger's postulate according to which an essential tendency toward closeness lies at the heart of Dasein. If coexistence engenders existence, human beings are "creatures who inhabited and administered a sphere" (SII 47). Dasein's spatiality, as uncovered by Heidegger, shows that human space is not to be confused with physical space as the a priori parameter of situated objects. Rather, it is defined as the a priori existential aspect of Dasein, which both produces and is a product of its own space:

> Space is not in the subject, nor is the world in space. Space is rather "in" the world in so far as space has been disclosed by that Being-in-the-world which is constitutive for Dasein. Space is not to be found in the subject, nor does the subject observe the world "as if" that world were in a space; but the subject (Dasein), if well understood ontologically, is spatial. And because Dasein is spatial in the way we have described, space shows itself as a priori. This term does not mean anything like previously belonging to a subject which is proximally still worldless and which emits a space out of itself. Here "apriority" means the previousness with which space has been encountered (as a region) whenever the ready-to-hand is encountered environmentally.[2]

In Sloterdijk's view, Heidegger's contribution convincingly shows that human space calls for a philosophical understanding of its spatiality (ontological side). Although this analytic pathway remains poorly exploited – despite the fact that it is ready to hand – it should also allow for a concrete analysis of human habitat as the organization of existence (anthropological side). In line with this desire to clarify the clearing and to break with Heidegger's empirical blindness, Bruno Latour believes that it is necessary to trivialize Dasein's relationship with space:

> Peter [Sloterdijk] asks his master Heidegger the rather mischievous questions: "When you say Dasein is thrown into the world, where is it thrown? What's the temperature there, the color of the walls, the material that has been chosen, the technology for disposing of refuse, the cost of the air-conditioning, and so on?" Here the apparently deep philosophical ontology of "Being qua Being" takes a rather different turn. Suddenly we realize that it is the "pro-found question" of Being that has been too superficially considered: Dasein has no clothes, no habitat, no biology, no hormones, no atmosphere around it, no medication, no viable transportation system even to reach his Hütte in the Black Forest. Dasein is thrown into the world but is so naked that it doesn't stand much chance of survival.[3]

Sloterdijk nevertheless places spherology under Heidegger's aegis and summarizes what is entailed by Heideggerian thinking about Dasein's spatiality:

> The concept of space used here is clearly non-physical, non-trivial and non-geometric, to the extent that, as Heidegger's very sombre remark shows, it must be older than all the usual dimensionalities, older in any event than the familiar three-dimensionality in which geometry represents spatial coordinates in the system of places. (NG 172)

However, in describing the paths that he plans to take, Sloterdijk argues that this philosophy of space must now exploit its analytic impulses and make Heidegger's ontological intuitions more concrete. In this connection, the concept of the sphere bridges the gap between ontology and anthropology by drawing out the concreteness of human beings' non-physical spatiality:

> I proposed the expression "sphere" to designate this non-trivial space to show how the organization of the original dimensionality can be conceived. Spheres are sites of inter-animal and interpersonal resonance within which the gathering of living beings engenders a plastic power. This power is such that the form of coexistence can go so far as to alter the very physiology of its co-inhabitants . . . These spherical localities, which at the outset are simply gatherings of animals, can be compared to greenhouses in which living creatures flourish in particular climatic conditions. In our case, the greenhouse effect goes so far as to encompass

ontological consequences: it can be plausibly shown how a being-in-the-greenhouse animal could become a being-in-the-world human. (NG 172–3)

As such, a recuperation of Heideggerian phenomenology could lead us to revisit the spaces of humanity, which have been subsumed for too long by metaphysics and are now broken apart by the globalization and infinite mobilization of capital. If spherology is the method by which it is possible to increase the spacious dimensions of the world, it is because it considers and re-spatializes what world capitalism tends to neglect and de-spatialize. This way of thinking converges again with that of Latour: "There exists no place that can be said to be 'non-local'. If something is to be 'delocalized', it means that it is being sent from one place to some other place, not from one place to no place."[4] The task for spherology is thus one of relocalizing the global.

Despite this promising or heretical reading of Heidegger that seeks to situate him at the forefront of thought about technology and spatiality,[5] it seems clear that space is a late arrival in the realm of high theory, which has traditionally focused only on abstractions of time. Because philosophers make up for lost ground by poetically and pompously recopying, in the manner of medieval scribes, "pagan sciences" (geography, anthropology, architecture, urbanism, and design), the interest of spherology stems perhaps from the fact that it obliges philosophy to return to being geocentric, if not geodesic.

To summarize the narrative of this long history and to evoke an image of the way to come, let us say that it is entirely contained in the metaphor of uterine destiny. It is a "poetics of natality"[6] to which Sloterdijk invites us in what he refers to as a "psycho-topo-immunology, a.k.a. the Spheres project, from 1998 to 2004" (ZT 281). Uterine destiny – the artificial, social construction of the incubating sphere found in the mother's womb – is not a state of symbiosis and immunization which we must forever renounce, as argued by the pessimistic Freud of *Civilization and Its Discontents*. On the contrary, it must be constantly emulated and rearticulated at various levels within the trajectory of our improbable species, which has become so artificial that it has to incubate itself without help from on high.

Spherological history takes form in a 2,500-page opus, which makes it difficult to manage and absolutely impossible to summarize.[7] In a fictive and caustic dialogue that colors the very end of this tale, Sloterdijk even amuses himself by imagining the reception of *Spheres* by means of a debate involving a theologian, a macrohistorian, and a literary critic. In the megalo-Nietzschean manner of self-commentary, we read that the very large volume of words contained in this project render it "ideologically irrecoverable and that from its very terminological surface, spherology is already a dissuasive element against

everything tending towards seriousness, power and audience ratings
. . . It will not take hold of the masses: academics already feel a malaise,
the neo-serious grimace, and unions express objections when they hear
it being talked about" (SIII 866).

This textual mass nevertheless evokes three preliminary observations. Firstly, it is not surprising that Sloterdijk resorts to enumeration
and illustration, given that the movement toward space has a ruinous
effect on high theory. The spatial and its "theorization" entail a radically empirical attitude, which could be understood as the real destination of the old phenomenological project, that is, teasing out an art of
writing that is at the service of experience. Is not the spatial turn,
spoken about since the 1980s, by means of the cumulative effect of
disciplines that "emphasize the materiality of thinking about and
exploring the possibility of a new a-whereness," another way of naming
this return to objects themselves?[8] To be sure, this new turn makes up
for a "lag" in big theory that had been unduly prolonged by the old
reflex of philosophers to dismiss space. If philosophers of Sloterdijk's
ilk are now "discovering" space, it is perhaps because philosophy's
thousand-year-old resistance became untenable as the geographical
question could no longer be ignored.

Secondly, while Sloterdijk's spatial turn is not original, its interest
lies in the fact that he steadfastly maintains his position on a fairly tight
crossing between "ontologization" and "explicitation."

Ontologization	**Explicitation**
Setting humans in an	*Making manifest the latent*
original spatiality	*characteristics of human habitats*

To appear simultaneously in these two prescriptive/descriptive cells,
he writes a great deal and manages to suggest a spatial ontology
without using any means other than the multiplication and reiteration
of sensual images that move us away both from Heideggerian stylistic
habits and weighty prose and from early onto-phenomenology. This
desire to make space explicit in such a way as to exhaust the manifestations of spherical reason eventually requires readers to immerse themselves in the spherological narrative, which, if it accomplishes the task
of a genuine bildungsroman, will transform one's self-perception into
"being-in-spheres."

Thirdly, this literary exploit is the fruit of an author-oracle. Through
him, the rich contributions of spatial sciences are brought together as
he *sensualizes* and synthesizes them in a long narrative. Referring to
Sloterdijk the spherologist as an oracle is tantamount to saying, with a
touch of irony, that he is an unequaled philosophical storyteller and
that this kind of inimitable tale can be told only once.

Once Upon a Time There Were Spheres

Sloterdijk tested this spherological hypothesis for the first time in an early political essay (see ISB) that can be seen as a kind of "pocket spherology." In it, although he already deploys the tripartite logic of his thinking,[9] he does so as a function less of a gradation of spherological reason than of forms of political aggregations. From the paleo-primitive to the hyper-complex aggregations, the development of spheres always operates in terms of a transference (*Übertragung*) of proven capacities for success in a small habitat to the promising capacities of emulation in a larger habitation project. Taking once more a road initially traced by Freud, *Im selben Boot* (*In the Same Boat*) uses this spherical transference thesis to account for the history of political constructions, the expectations engendered by projects intended to increase the size of the common habitat, and the violence brought on by the collapse of fragile or temporary "incubators" (see following paragraphs) that could no longer guarantee a pacifying sphere effect. Indeed, the massacres carried out in the early 1990s in the former Yugoslavia serve as a backdrop for this discussion of the imperatives of the construction of pacifying psychopolitical entities: "Interpreting the major deregulation movements in the Balkans (as well as in the republics in the Caucasus, Africa and other crisis zones) as consequences of political stress stemming from the new world order also entails an examination from a political perspective of the forms likely to defuse this stress" (ISB 62). To this end, Sloterdijk proposes an examination of three sets of political constitutions that have been developed over the long course of human time: paleo-politics, classical politics, and hyper-politics.

Arguing against the narrative of the originally political or civilized *Humanitas*, Sloterdijk notes that more than 98 percent of human history has taken place within the framework of psychopolitical microforms that were sub-state, sub-pharaonic, and sub-civilization constitutions for coexistence. Even better, these primitive spheres – called paleo-political – are the only ones that can lay claim to having given birth to *Homo sapiens* via a process of insulating the hordes who were gradually taken out of nature: "These groups can be viewed as social islands to the extent that they effectively emerge out of their environment as animated spheres and because they are surrounded by an invisible ring of distantiation that liberates human bodies from the constraints of the old nature" (ISB 17). Sloterdijk argues that the paleo-politics of the hordes accomplished the "miracle of the reproduction of human beings for human beings," to the extent that they were the first form of successful "incubator": "The hordes are groups of human beings incubating other human beings and transmitting the qualities of an always-at-risk luxury to their descendants over extremely vast periods of time" (ISB 19). In sum, the most durable political form – paleo-political islands – warrants our attention because it is the oldest form of human coexistence and, precisely for this reason, contains the secrets of the human womb's incubating function. Sloterdijk borrows this favorite formula once again from Dieter Claessens: "The womb is a social space since it signifies nothing other than assuming the protective functions ensured by internal maternal space, turned here, however, towards the outside. This external space would be impossible had it not existed beforehand. It is for this reason that it is permissible to call it the 'social womb.'"[10] All the more extensive and more complex political orders that followed – without ever abolishing it – have found a way to emulate the production of this primitive concord via an "acoustic bubble":

> Like their successors in the order of culture, the primitive hordes socialize their members in a psycho-spherical and sono-spherical continuum in which existence and belonging are almost inseparable entities. The oldest society is a marvellous little chattering bubble – an invisible circus tent suspended above and moving with the troupe. Each individual is linked more or less continuously with the group's resonance chamber by way of psycho-acoustic umbilical cords. (ISB 21)

This metaphor of musical harmony designates the "common self-tuning of the group by means of the ear" (SIII 381). It can be reproduced and extended from micro-political hordes to the largest groups of *coexistents*. Thus, the succeeding age of classical politics inherited the task of "reproducing the older horde's miraculous psycho-acoustic bubble, though at the level of the world and the cosmos" (ISB 34). The large agricultural civilizations of this second age successfully projected the primitive onto a larger scale to the extent that they conceived of the state, this "metaphorical mother," as a means of artificial political acclimatization that succeeded in maintaining the unity of the many through the fantasy of the community of citizens: "This kind of political hyper-horde was meant to be a larger variation of the configuration of the social womb to the extent that it created a total group out of a multiplicity of hordes, houses, families and clans. According to Plato, politics remains, to a certain extent, merger management or work on the imaginary hyper-womb for political children" (ISB 36). In its more universalizing forms (Stoic and soon thereafter Christian), the age of agri-classical politics exceeded the fragmented structure of alliances between city-states and embraced a global form that radiated from the centrality of universal reason or a single divinity. "It is from the centre that the contours of the world are drawn; from an ontological perspective, it is the invisible bubble of entities that takes shape around God, the single Being whose effects are felt by all; from a cosmological point of view, it is a luminous sphere; from a political point of view, it is the world ring organized around a centre of domination" (ISB 43–4).

The age of classical politics and its large imperial conglomerations lasted until the birth of industrial societies, which led to unprecedented global mobilization. The dissolution of older regimes to the benefit of the bourgeois world created a point of rupture that brought the classical age face to face with its new incapacities and took the form of a challenge for all future political regimes.

In Sloterdijk's view, the death of God became the central determining element of attempts at establishing a postclassical political order, which were forced to bear in mind the organizational consequences of this major disappearance: "Proclaiming the death of God in a culture conditioned by monotheism entails a shake-up of all systems of relations and announces a new kind of world" (ISB 50). It can be said that the third political age inherited the projection into the Big from the preceding age, but without its guarantees and certainties – it was no longer able to name the "something" that served to ground the union of the Sons of the One. Nevertheless, it continued its world conquest, not from an expanding center but by way of synchronizing the circulation of capital in a "wired hyper-bubble" (ISB 21).

Although the age of classical politics had managed to produce its "state athletes," those who succeeded in incarnating, maintaining, and ensuring the credibility of the older political orders' performative fiction, Sloterdijk raises certain questions about the present-day possibility of recruiting the hyper-athletes needed for a credible hyper-politics – a politics of the global that can reduce local stress. Given that no political actors appear to be able to deal with current challenges and the consequent "crises of disgust felt by current society for its own politicians" (ISB 54), Sloterdijk intends to seize the opportunity to reflect upon the current possibilities for creating a new world-pacifying form. The current crisis has reached the point where the stress felt by populations, brutally exposed to the logic of the Big, threatens to spread throughout the entire empire of globalization:

> *Homo sapiens*, a small-group animal, will be overwhelmed by large civilization for as long as it does not manage to create the symbolic and emotional prostheses that will enable it to flourish in the Big . . . Societies which even recently resembled almost integrated civilizations could revert to the stage of neurotic tribes following the loss of imaginary political prostheses. (ISB 60)

The apparent failure of the current form of the hyper-political incubator thus calls for a fundamental review of the motives underlying a human association that can measure up to the situation. In this regard, Sloterdijk's prescriptions vacillate between two distinct avenues that fully reveal the extent of his ambivalence toward the crises and hopes of hyper-politics. In a twofold movement of disaggregation and aggregation, Sloterdijk charts the two paths upon which hyper-political efforts could lead either to a return to the Small (which he presents as the rebirth of small-scale association) or to completely new large-scale constructions (which he identifies in a related work as the hopes of the European construction).[11]

Im selben Boot clearly favors the promises of the first path, which should serve as a clue to the political preferences of the coming spherology. In this connection, Sloterdijk takes his inspiration from Boccaccio's *Decameron*, a collection of tales depicting the tribulations of a group of survivors who withdrew from the city to protect themselves from the Florentine plague, which Sloterdijk describes as "a pedagogical treatise instructive of the relationship between regenerative gaiety and small-scale politics" (ISB 65). The theme of retreat is celebrated as a means of perpetuating human association in times when large cities fail to accomplish this elementary task: "By their disaggregation, superstructures reveal that they have practically nothing to offer to individuals who are making an effort to perpetuate life. It thus seems clear that when the opus commune disaggregates at larger scales, small units are the only framework likely to enable human beings to regenerate" (ISB 64). The fact of giving birth does not require *Große Politik* (Big Politics). The Epicurean act, consisting in recreating the enclosure of a healthy, sustainable microcity at the heart of deteriorating large-scale citizen life, thus combines with an *Urpolitics* – original political order – that humanity has maintained and honored for the greater part of its history.

Sloterdijk's ternary schematic, the elements of which are revisited and discussed in depth in the works making up the *Spheres* trilogy, reveals that large constructions can succeed only if they never forget to acknowledge the role of associative sub-entities. Indeed, the latter provide them with a credible existence so long as they are preserved and aggregated in a larger organizational order. The long history of spherical constructions, from the most intimate to the most global in nature, reveals that the secret of contemporary harmony also lies at some point on the boundary between aggregation and disaggregation.

A streetcar named Great Narratives

The outlines of this first formulation of the spherological transference hypotheses are maintained in the much more ambitious *Spheres* project. Indeed, though the ternary schematic remains intact, it casts aside the terms paleo-, classical, and hyper-politics and resolutely gives form to a much richer human spatiality (architectural, literary, and pictorial). For Sloterdijk, the metaphor of the sphere is the means of updating this spatiality, which calls for a threefold inquiry – microspherological, macrospherological, and plurispherological – into the three gradients of spherological reason (bubbles, globes, and foams) that are used to explain human spaces.

For the purposes of a brief presentation, let us hop on a streetcar named Great Narratives for a quick trip into the great interior of spherological reason. Inside this streetcar, a large, semicircular sofa surrounds our author-oracle who, though his back is turned to the audience, performs what Niklas Luhmann (a sociologist critical of critical theory and much appreciated by Sloterdijk) calls observation of observation.[12] The streetcar's route will take it backwards in time and, with the help of a voluble oracle, tell us what is being explained (i.e. made explicit, shown or demonstrated, *monstratum*) in the surrounding landscape. The streetcar will go back into the spatial age, from the most sophisticated to the most primitive, by moving along a line with three stations: crystal palace, constructions in the colossal, and the birth of anthropogenic insulations.

Foams, crystal palace, indulgences   The streetcar is in the middle of a crystal palace. This immense glass and steel structure covers a vast, luxurious, peaceful, and air-conditioned interior, the civilizational scope of which had already been foreseen by Dostoyevsky in *Notes from the Underground.*[13] This first stop is in fact the terminal of the long history of the conquest of the comfortable life by a small minority of human beings. As the ultimate container and "emblem for the final ambitions of modernity" (WIC 176), the crystal palace became, following the phases of imperialist expansion that accompanied the birth of terrestrial globalization, the great indoors of capitalism that guaranteed pleasure only for the chosen while keeping the wretched and their misery outside its crystal bubble. Earlier expansionist and colonizing movements have given way to a reverse movement of retraction that concentrates and consolidates wealth in the metropolitan island of global players, who build gated communities on a national scale: "The world interior of capital is not an agora or a trade fair beneath the open sky, but rather a hothouse that has drawn inwards everything that was once on the outside. The bracing climate of an integral inner world of commodity can be formulated in the notion of a planetary palace of consumption" (WIC 12). This internal, pacified organization must not be confused with universal or perpetual peace in that it relies on the presence of barbed wire, walls, borders, watchtowers, and patrols to control who enters the palace, above which can be heard the whoosh of drones and supersonic fighters on permanent alert.

The streetcar slowly gets underway. As it moves along its route, we get a broader view of the activities and kinds of habitations that make up this large hothouse of advanced capitalism. The crystal palace is governed by two linked principles: antigravity and indulgence. These principles support the coming to power of the following words: pacification, safety, abundance, and frivolity. In spherological or climatic terms, it corresponds to the age of foams, which is the lightest and airiest form of spherical habitat, given that life in foams means primarily that lightness overthrows heaviness. In foams, the primacy of the gaseous over the solid (the earth of the ancient native land) and the liquid (modern conquering navigation) metaphorically designates this mutation of material and mental states, no longer in phase with the traditional discourse of political economy (need) and the sacrificial discourse of political engagement (suffering). However, there is nothing unexpected about the emergence of great luxury. On the contrary, argues Sloterdijk, the reasons for living luxuriously are as old as the human species. Indeed, the long history of the onto-anthropological propensity for luxury is based initially on the reason for the existence of human constructions. The first circle of large primates clearly sought to rid itself of the weight of the natural environment through the creation of a comfortable inhabitable world. The history of luxury is the history of relief, two concepts that Sloterdijk had thought about before his spherological project:

> Luxury makes humankind possible, and it is through luxury that our world is born. Since the very beginning, humans have been animals that offer each other relief by watching over one another and by giving themselves more security than any other living creature could ever dream of having . . . Humankind emerged by breaking free of Mother Nature. The birth of humankind can be told in terms of the spirit of vigilance. (WF 334)

What the crystal palace and the proliferation of the foam habitat make explicit is the age-old tendency of humans to mutually unburden and exonerate one another. Simply stated, they offer the gift of relief to one another.[14] In Sloterdijk's view, relief entails that the inquiry be developed through an explicit acceptance of a "theory of constitutive luxury" (SIII 676), to conceptualize the point of origin and of arrival of human history. To this end, he proposes the use of the term *Verwöhnung* (pampering), which in German is etymologically related to *Wohnung* (habitation): "Pampering, as a term from historical anthropology, denotes the psychophysical and semantic reflexes of the relieving process that was inherent in the civilization process from the start, but could only become fully visible in the age of a radical de-scarcification of goods" (WIC 212).

When the streetcar reaches its cruising speed in the interior of the large consumer greenhouse, Sloterdijk resorts to satire to caricature the excesses and discontents found in the society of comfort. To do so, he describes the five stages of relief in the crystal palace's society of overabundance:

> [T]he interior of the postmodern crystal palace contains an elevator that transports residents to the five expansively constructed floors of relief . . . The first floor is for those who have succeeded in partially or completely fulfilling the dream of income without performance; the second is frequented by an audience of relaxed citizens who profit from political security without themselves having any readiness to fight; the third is where those meet who participate in general provisions of immunity without having their own history of suffering; on the fourth, consumers of a knowledge whose acquisition requires no experience spread themselves out; and on the fifth one finds those who, through direct publication of their own person, have succeeded in becoming famous without presenting any achievements or publishing any work. (WIC 213)

In traveling throughout the crystal palace's vast regions, the oracle leaves the terrain of sarcasm and the received critique of consumer society (and the generalization of wealth that accompanies it and that has been a source of ire to noble spirits since Tocqueville), and focuses his attention more seriously on the description of the kind of habitation corresponding to present-day antigravity. This descriptive task is tackled in *Schäume* (*Foams*), the last tome of *Spheres*, and also finds an echo in *In the World Interior of Capital*.[15]

The route continues as it goes through downtown areas, university campuses, industrial parks, amusement parks, bedroom communities, and huge housing towers. In crossing through these areas, Sloterdijk seeks to describe the birth of a completely new kind of "society" or social connectivity by means of the foam metaphor, the subtlest and most fragile of spherical constructions. What are foams? Drawing on the spherological hypothesis, Sloterdijk argues that in light of the implosion of the Christian monosphere, smaller, inferior spheres have the task of emulating the monosphere's immunological functions via a foamy composition of a disarticulated social architecture. As such, foams "are agglomerations of bubbles, . . . systems or aggregates of spherical neighbourhoods within which each 'cell' constitutes a self-complementing context" (SIII 55). Foams are the lightest and most portable form of spherical habitat, an airy structure that meets the minimum encapsulation condition of human beings "living together." The operative principle of foams is "co-isolation plus aggregation," an associative rule that could lead the way to a renewed understanding of social configurations:

> By "society," we designate an aggregate of microspheres of varying sizes (couples, houses, enterprises, associations, etc.) linked together like bubbles in a mountain of foam, which slide over or under the

others without ever being attainable by or detachable from one another.
(SIII 59)

Such is the principle of "isolated connectivity" that links together the
insulated particles making up contemporary societies. This principle
recalls Gabriel Tarde's monadological intuitions in the late nineteenth
century: "Each one [of the material elements], formerly viewed as a
point, becomes an indefinitely enlarged sphere of action; . . . and all
these interpenetrating spheres are so many domains specific to each
element, perhaps so many distinct, if mixed spaces, that we falsely take
to be a single space."[16]

Continuing his examination of this multiple space composed of
linked compartments, Sloterdijk defines three forms of isolation produced by human beings, and which have been made particularly
explicit by modern and contemporary capacities for building artificial
islands: absolute islands, atmospheric islands, and anthropogenic
islands. Absolute islands, like spacecraft, airplanes, and space stations,
are the most radical forms of insulation. They must guarantee by
themselves an internal environment favorable to life while surrounded
by a hostile, if not lethal, outside environment. To a lesser extent,
atmospheric islands, such as greenhouses or settings for artificial life,
are relatively isolated from their terrestrial environment. They emulate
simplified real ecological systems while remaining permeable to the
external environment. For their part, anthropogenic islands (self-iso-
lating environments or self-incubators that take care of human beings)
vacillate between the absolute and the atmospheric island models. As
genuine avenues for spatial analysis, anthropogenic islands cut across
a series of equally varied and complex sites and represent just as
many variations on the theme of the humanization process's spatial
variables. With a view to systematizing his approach to these analytic
avenues, at the end of the first chapter of *Schäume*, Sloterdijk proposes
a typology that designates the anthroposphere's nine sites: chiroptope
(domain accessible by hand); phonotope (vocal bell under which co-
inhabitants listen to one another); uteroptope (maternal zone and its
first social metaphorizations); thermotope (warm circle of comfort);
erototope (primary erotic energy transfer zone); ergotope (shared
spirit of cooperation in common labor); alethotope (continuity of the
collective worldview); thanatope (space of revelation for elders and
gods); and nomotope (social architecture and its political constitution).
These anthropogenic islands are intended as promising avenues for
future inquiry into the worldly spatiality of humans as insulated
creatures.

Sloterdijk's analysis draws out the productiveness of his typology
in his in-depth empirical study of the contemporary forms of habitats
that, for the first time in human history, enabled the generalization of

the single-individual cell model. Beginning with the observation that "the inhabitants of modern, media-sustained houses have already replaced the vague psycho-semantic protection systems provided by religious metaphysics with their highly-specialized and legally- and climatically-insulated habitation cells which are assisted by anonymous systems of solidarity" (SIII 540), Sloterdijk argues that present-day apartments are on the point of taking on "an atomic or elementary egospheric form – as a cellular world-bubble, the massive repetition of which generates individualistic foams" (SIII 569).[17] In a precise immunospherical sense, living in foams now means living in a self-referencing living capsule that "serves [the inhabitant] as the stage for his self-pairing, as the operating room for his self-care, and as an immune system in a highly contaminated field of connected isolations, also known as neighborhoods" (SIII 576).[18]

At times, the observation of these self-sustaining luxury containers leads Sloterdijk to wonder about the possibility of seeing these new forms of anthropogenic islands imitate the absolute island model. This would involve such an extent of closure and self-sufficiency that their inhabitants would be completely cut off from the world. The spread of self-referential bubbles could indicate the danger inherent in the principle of isolated connectivity, namely that it is less likely to link than to divide. This avenue could even make it possible for modern individualism to recover a much darker meaning, despite the fact that Sloterdijk denounces the fiction of the self-generated subject, against which the spherological undertaking argues (see chapter 5).

The oracle's discourse is interrupted by the sudden appearance of a signal light in the landscape through which the streetcar is traveling. This panel flashes above the tunnel that leads us to the second stop on the streetcar's route, and in bright electronic letters it clamours: "Attention! God is Dead."

Globes, constructions in the colossal, metaphysics   As our eyes adjust themselves to the tunnel's darkness, Sloterdijk establishes a link between the habitation issue and that of the death that has been announced.

> The sentence "God is dead" is confirmed as the good news of our times. We could reformulate it: Sphere-One has imploded; long live the foams . . . To say that the harmful God of consensus is dead is to acknowledge the energy with which we take up the work . . . When a great exaggeration has outlived itself, swarms of more discreet upswings emerge. (SIII 26)

If the foams that inhabit the crystal palace appear to obey the law of minimal coherence and unity, it is because they are the product of an immunological reaction. Foams are manifestations of plural spherology, which is a response to the crisis induced by the end of macrospherological orders and seeks to account for a mutation in the order of immunological prostheses. Foams once again take up the task of producing and incubating human beings, during which time thousands of years of monospherical care work are dissipated. In this regard, what Sloterdijk had already written in *Im selben Boot* is fully maintained in the spherological perspective: God is the principle and guarantor of constructions in the great order of things. In his absence, these guarantees no longer exist and anthropotechnical work necessarily operates on a smaller scale. In the age we have just left, this renewed swarm is called the microspherology of foams.

The tunnel taking us to the constructions in the colossal is partially lighted as the streetcar crosses through a dusty museum. In this museum, we can see piled pell-mell a collection of very ancient coins, of globus crucigers (cross-bearing orbs), and old, solemn paintings of pagan or Christian monarchs and emperors with a hand or foot on globes that serve to metamorphose their great power, that is, "the meaning of totality of the classical sphere" (SII 55).[19] One of the museum's most important pieces is a statue depicting Atlas holding the heavy celestial sphere on his shoulders. These artefacts from another time are instantly recuperated within the general economy of the oracle's discourse: globalization is a very ancient form of "spheropoeise" (SII 48), the production of spheres, which is the product of a long history. Current globalization discourses lend no credence to this history and to these origins. It is for this reason that spherology claims the status of the "true narrative" of globalization on the basis of its "true origin":

> Therefore, the starting date of the original globalization can be determined, at least as an epoch, with some clarity: it is the cosmological enlightenment of the Greek thinkers who, combining ontology with geometry, brought the great sphere into play. (SII 50)[20]

The inaugural fascination of a handful of ancient Athenians with spherical perfection resulted in the fact that "mathematical globalization precedes terrestrial globalization by more than two thousand years" (SII 48). Since Sloterdijk likes to annul time in favor of space, the permanence of spherical geometry pushes him to say that modern cosmology is less a rupture than a kind of bastardized extension of ancient cosmology's pure, abstract institutions. It is again in this sense that current globalization is viewed as a vulgar or disgusting version of spherology: it impoverishes being-in-the-spheres and does not rise above the earth's crust, which is no longer anything more than a "last orb" (SII 801; WIC 14). Sloterdijk thus draws a distinction between metaphysical globalization and modern circumnavigation, which is no more than terrestrial globalization. By the same token, the spherical totality is impoverished by the conquest of the world as a picture (terrestrial sphere), which, according to Heidegger, is "the fundamental event of modernity" (SII 47).[21] Just before leaving the museum, which had suddenly emerged in the middle of the tunnel, we spy a detail in a modern painting showing the hand of Elizabeth I of England lying not on a globus cruciger or a sphere of wisdom, but on a naked, round earth overlaid with meridians and trade routes.

The streetcar now enters a gigantic landscape filled as far as the eye can see with the architectural megalomania associated with the age of globes. The oracle notes that this second major moment of spherology can be viewed as a "reasoned history of metaphysics" (ZT 309), that is, an age of colossal constructions that translated the spirit of cosmic totalization and strong simplification into bricks and concrete.[22] To understand this novel link between colossal architecture and metaphysics, it must be recalled that spherical construction obeys that law of transference: expansion projects are possible only if they are based on the success of earlier, smaller projects. In the case of globes, the success of this transference is leveraged by the mad ambition of metaphysics or of the God hypothesis in which there is no limit to the enveloping universality of the cosmic sphere. Taken in its ultimate sense, the age of globes is an extraordinary projection in the Big that contrasts with the retraction movement observed in the crystal palace of the foams. Here, an extroverted globe expands to the same extent as the faith in Atlas, the only and total principle that serves as guarantor. The age of globes believes in the existence of a fixed, luminous center from which points on the periphery receive their share of light and their relative coordinates. It corresponds to what was referred to earlier as the age of agri-classical politics.

Any immuno-spherological revolution entails a transference of an older, "obsolete" sphere's immunological properties to a new sphere that extends it – such is the formula by which spheres evolve, change, and articulate the various geodesic strata of spatial experiences. Walls, arks, temples, domes, and pantheons are the oldest forms of architectural *globisolation*, which provided the experience of internal islands meant to autonomously ensure a spherical effect that made them more habitable than the larger outside world. As an example of an ideal type of this isolation and insulation principle, Sloterdijk argues that Noah's Ark demonstrates a human-made sphere that constitutes "an absolute, decontextualized and autonomous house, a construction without a neighborhood that incarnates by itself the negation of the environment by means of its artificial structure" (SII 251). Noah's Ark not only gives explicit form to the idea that we are always in the same boat, but also illustrates one of the possibilities and the most critical conditions of spherological purpose, namely that of ensuring by itself all of the requirements of a habitat that must reproduce life.

The Ark is the symptom of a macro-globular drive supporting a totalizing spherical habitation capacity. Still, one wonders whether the oracle gets a bit caught up in his own words and comes himself to believe in the language of these outrageous simplifications and their "holistic spells."[23] Although we cannot always make out what he is saying, the oracle deals successively with the ontology of the orb, amphitheaters, or Nicholas de Cusa's *De ludo globi*, and winds up exasperating a few passengers whose ears are getting a bit sore: "he is not ready at any time to abandon *Grand Style* metaphysics."[24]

Indeed, *Globes* and, even more, *In the World Interior of Capital* offer a narrative of the fall from globular metaphysics. While applauding the age of ancient extroverted spheres, Sloterdijk illustrates ad nauseam the expansion process by which this "interior community" domesticates the global. Yet in contrast to this metaphysically enchanted age of a vaulted, mothered earth, the European expansion (1492–1945) – the first wave of the impoverishment of globalization – trades the metaphysician for the mapmaking navigator whose primary task is to remanufacture the world's image. Thenceforth, human beings were solely interested in the surface of the earth and its naked crust. While homogenizing space, the mapping enterprise is delocalizing all spatial coordinates and rendering them relative only to others. These flattened, naked places are then estranged from the former inclusive, mother-like landscape cosmogony. Indeed, each point on the earth's surface becomes a relay station, a temporary outpost for further global exploration, that is, "a potential address for the Capital" (SII 828). This terrestrial globalization, understood as total mobilization over water, is not an "age of great discoveries," but, rather, an age in which navigators have exported a "loco-motivated" Europe (SII 835) that has been able to carry its spatiality overseas through the prototypical figure of vessels that have sustained a "corporate identity on high seas" (SII 877). Modern entrepreneurship prays to chance (Fortuna) and displays tolerance for calculated risks. Since the main issue of modern globalization turns on investments on which one anticipates a return, Sloterdijk's ironic argument is that "the main fact of Modern times is not that the earth goes round the sun, but that money goes round the earth" (SII 856).

Terrestrial globalization comes to an end five centuries later. After 1945, the last phase of the "disgusting" reduction of the world becomes an inhibited and secured age that seeks only to consolidate the great indoors of capitalism, which was what the oracle had precisely described in the characteristics of the crystal palace. Venturing and risking follow the present eventless "epoch," also described as posthistory: "Post-historical situations are those in which historical actions (religious foundations, crusades, revolutions, liberation wars, class struggles, with all their heroic and fundamental aspects) are forbidden because of their incalculable risks" (SII 900). To illustrate this contrast between history (as unilateral) and posthistory (as inhibited), Sloterdijk argues that America's colonization shows that "the one that would be considered a criminal in juridical or post-historical times is seen rather as a hero in the turbulence of history" (SII 945–6). And this double standard makes Sloterdijk believe that perhaps terrestrial "globalization, just as history, is a crime that can be committed only once" (SII 947).

To stress the contrast between the age of globes and the age of foams, the oracle recaps the narrative of the shift between the two: the "last globe" encompasses privileged surfaces and archipelagos of the earth's crust with an affluent habitat built on electronic capitalist networks. "The last globe still allows horizontal constructions . . . but it daunts any thoughts for a Super-monosphere or for a ruling center of all centers" (SII 995). Yet the disappearance of a global center of power reveals that the age of great holisms has been replaced with an amorphous and complex order that carries the symptoms of another great immuno-spherical transformation. A passenger at the back of the car asks: "Are the foams an outcome of a more primitive spherology?" As the oracle turns to answer the question, the car's lights suddenly go off, as do the discreet hums of the electric motor and the air conditioning. A few passengers light the car's small interior with candles or their lighters. A voice announces: "Attention! You are now leaving the territory of history." The tramway's rails disappear into a cave that swallows the car.

Bubbles, birth of anthropogenic insulations, childhood Without the light of our small flames, we would be in total darkness. This radical change of atmosphere silences the passengers. This prehistoric tunnel appears to be very, very long, clearly much longer than all the distance covered so far since the crystal palace station, already a distant memory. The major exaggeration of the celestial and metaphysical constructions contrasts to such an extent with the darkness of the moment that it no longer sheds any light on the present situation. A small group and their oracle drift beyond the continent of history and retrace the strand of spherological reason to its Paleolithic point of origin.

The glowing objects we carry are enough to shed light on the rocky walls that slide by as we go backwards in time. In the cave, large stretches of flat walls are at times brightened by paintings of large wild animals. Daylight finally pierces the darkness and makes the passengers squint. During the voyage, these same passengers had huddled together to concentrate the strength of their light sources and to reinvigorate themselves by way of close contact with their neighbors

sharing the same adventure. As the streetcar leaves the tunnel, a primitive village and a circle made by a few hunters drawn up around a fire
can be seen not far away from the cave.

The silence is broken by the oracle's whispering. The projection into
the Big, it repeats, did not create *Homo sapiens*. The three-part narrative
of spherology begins rather on a primitive or even obstetric terrain:
human beings produce and incubate themselves. According to the gra-
dations depicted in *Im selben Boot*, the oldest kind of organization of
the species was paleo-politics, the oldest form of human coexistence.
However, the microspherology discussed in *Bubbles*, says the oracle,
leaves aside the Paleolithic field, which is concerned rather with work
devoted to anthropotechnics (chapter 2). The study of the smallest
spherological unit is confronted instead with the issue of birth and
intra-uterine intimacy. Although the streetcar has stopped in the middle
of the Paleolithic Period, the spherological journey is not yet over.

For the end of the narrative, the oracle will use the language of
midwives and explore the microspherology of the retreat within the
mother, the egg principle, or the fate of the placenta as a discarded
organ. This gynecological exploration is intended as a "phenomenological expedition through the formal sequence of bipolar closeness
and intimacy spheres" (B 280), for which fetal inhabitation of the
mother counts among "the most intimate and historically profound
interpretation[s] conceivable of the spherical union between subjects"
(B 246). It is microclimates such as these that are the starting point of
the oracle's grand narrative. The uterine intimacy between a mother
and child becomes the intimacy between their faces, which is then
enhanced by voice and speech, followed by all the other postnatal
transformations of this first welcome to the world. Microspheres are
variations on the same natal theme:

> We are in a microsphere whenever we are – *firstly* in the intercordial space
> – *secondly* in the interfacial sphere – *thirdly* in the field of "magical"
> binding forces and hypnotic effects of closeness – *fourthly* in immanence,
> that is to say in the interior of the absolute mother and its postnatal
> metaphorizations – *fifthly* in the co-dyad, or the placenta doubling and
> its successor – *sixthly* in the care of the irremovable companion and its
> metamorphoses – *seventhly* in the resonant space of the welcoming mater-
> nal voice and its messianic-evangelistic-artistic duplications. (B 540)

Incubating and giving birth constitute the first spherological exercise
and transference. All future habitation transferences depend upon the
microclimate of birth and childhood.

> As creatures that – under all circumstances – initially live towards
> one another, house and discard one another, and are nothing else beyond
> this, before possibly and much later, as so-called individuals, becoming

self-augmenting solitary dwellers who cultivate outside contacts (addresses, networks), humans are universally reliant on the supportive microclimates of their early internal worlds. Only within these, as their typical growths, do they become what they can be, whether it is beneficial or harmful to them. There they collect a store of creative, ambivalent and destructive undertones or emotional prejudices about the existent as a whole that stubbornly assert themselves in the transition to larger scenes. It is from this collection that all transferences initiate themselves.[25] (SII 143–4)

The inaugural scene of early childhood and the decisive nature of the microclimate that defines it make up a reservoir of enthusiasm or of pessimism that will be mobilized at every liminal moment in the conquest and the organization of our own living spaces.

The autosuggestive dream to which the streetcar's passengers have voluntarily abandoned themselves comes to an end. Although all of microspherology's therapeutic avenues have yet to be revealed (see chapter 5), we have a better understanding of what we announced before embarking on this journey. The uterine destiny is truly the heart of the spherological narrative: incubating oneself without help from on high. The intra-uterine habitat is the clearest illustration of the spherological postulate that coexistence precedes essence. Metaphorically transposed, this praise for the Small becomes the common denominator of various moments of a fable that recounts the long odyssey of human immunology on the way to becoming a planetary conscience and generalization:

Global immunitary reason is one step higher than all those things that its anticipation in philosophical idealism and religious monotheism were capable of attaining . . . It demands that one transcend all previous distinctions between own and foreign . . . This structure would take on planetary dimensions at the moment when the earth, spanned by networks and built over foams, was conceived as the own, and the previous dominant exploitative excess as the foreign. With this turn, the concretely universal would become operational. The helpless whole is transformed into a unity capable of being protected . . . Humanity becomes a political concept. Its members are no longer travellers on the ship of fools that is abstracted universalism, but workers on the consistently concrete and discrete project of a global immune design. (MCL 451)

4

Controversy

"There are only plausible and implausible arguments, creative and stagnant thoughts, courageous and cowardly reflections, plentiful and limited opinions, interesting and dull ways of writing."[1] This chapter discusses Sloterdijk's rise to prominence in Germany, including his conflicts with established German academia and his growing media presence. The *enfant terrible* often attacks philosophers who have no interest in stepping outside the strict purview of academic study; he wishes rather to embody an agonistic stance, inhibited by neither political sensitivity nor scholarly caution, that dares to publicly raise controversial questions.

This attitude put Sloterdijk in direct conflict and competition with fellow intellectuals Jürgen Habermas and Axel Honneth of the Frankfurt School. The 1999 Habermas–Sloterdijk controversy revolved around "Rules for the Human Zoo," which Habermas decried as being akin to Naziesque and eugenicist positions. This initial controversy was marked by Sloterdijk's subaltern position within German media circles vis-à-vis Habermas's European superstar status. A decade later, Sloterdijk dominated a second round of debates with the Frankfurt School, engaging Axel Honneth over the issue of taxation in post-necessity economies ("Die Revolution der gebenden Hand").[2] This clash was characterized by Sloterdijk's contemptuous disregard for his adversary, revealing the fact that Sloterdijk's status was no longer measured against the Frankfurt School's until-then hegemonic legitimacy.

Sloterdijk's major role as a public intellectual in contemporary Germany seems to exacerbate the strength of the rivalry between the intelligentsia and the media world, and probably even more so because he stands astride the border separating the two universes.[3] Well aware of the firm opposition between these two modes of intellectual production, Sloterdijk tries to avoid this rigidity by asserting that, in the final analysis, there are only interesting and uninteresting thoughts. Indeed, he often attacks philosophers who have no interest in descending the cloud-enshrouded steps of the ivory tower. This gap between the "celestial" inhabitants of pure academia and the "mundane" generalists of the public sphere ensures that genuine interaction between them remains impossible. In contradistinction to this "from-professors, to-professors" philosophy, Sloterdijk's Heinian-Nietzschean posture has highlighted the discontents in the German academic world, which traditionally "developed an inability to promote philosophy beyond the university [and had] no genuinely philosophical interest in mediating and communicating."[4] Struggling against this tendency, not only has Sloterdijk introduced stardom into philosophy, but he also seeks to reconcile his fellow citizens to the necessity of dissensual discourses, and to embody an agonistic position that overshadows any contending proponents of zero-sum declarations at zero personal cost. However, this heroic posture is not without a certain number of blind spots or political blunders, which perhaps reveal the philosopher's desire to become the prince's advisor, to trade in the nightingale's feathers for those of the hawk.

German *Publizistik*

Before examining the two controversies at the heart of this chapter, brief mention should be made of the editorial vehicles that characterized them in a specifically German manner. From the wasteland of the so-called zero years – from the surrender in 1945 to the 1949 promulgation of the Basic Law – until the return of the Federal Parliament (Bundestag) in Berlin in 1999, the German intellectual press was largely the theater of major national debates that helped shape the *Bonner Republik*'s political and intellectual history.

Indeed, during these decades, the coverage of German controversies in the cultural pages of the national *Intelligenzblätter* (intellectual gazette) served as a privileged vehicle for the genesis of major national polemics.[5] In addition to a polarized political context that fostered the need for these periodic bouts of soul-searching, West Germany could rely on ardent intellectual journalism characterized as much by its impact as by its quality: "There is a peculiar German tradition of *Publizistik* [intellectual journalism] with the *Publizist* writing in newspapers and magazines, while often not being a professional journalist, and publishing scholarly books, while not being an academic."[6] Among these well-known vehicles, the periodicals *Merkur* and *Kursbuch*, the newspapers *Frankfurter Allgemeine Zeitung*, *Süddeutsche Zeitung*, and *Die Zeit*, and the magazines *Der Spiegel*, *Focus*, and *Stern* trained intellectual agitators as well as other opinion leaders who have helped shape the contours of public debate in recent decades.[7] This mechanism had already been fine-tuned when the Sloterdijk Affair erupted in 1999, at a time when the political and philosophical fields appeared to transpose themselves onto one another in real time.

Struggle within Suhrkamp

One of the elements that colored the entire climate of the skirmish surrounding "Rules for the Human Zoo" in early 1999 was Sloterdijk's elevation to one of the highest positions in German academic publishing. Siegfried Unseld, head of Suhrkamp (the prominent publisher of the entire catalogue of critical theory and its successors), moved closer to the thinker whom he viewed as one of the most significant contemporary philosophers. To do so, he set out to enhance his long-term collaboration with established names such as Ulrich Beck and Jürgen Habermas by drawing on advice from Peter Sloterdijk. The news of this move was far from pleasing to proponents of the austere tradition of *Sachbücher* (academic and specialist writing), who feared the threats posed by the internal shifts entailed by what was announced as a necessary turning point in Suhrkamp's editorial policy. What would thenceforth be privileged would be "the essay as the main form of contemporary cultural theory."[8] Indeed, the very declaration of this shift reveals the full depth of Sloterdijk's stamp on this new culture.

As Heinz-Ulrich Nennen noted with a certain irony, Unseld was fully able "to go to lunch with Habermas on Monday, with Sloterdijk on Tuesday and with [Peter] Handke on Wednesday."[9] However, this intellectual and literary libertinage raised serious concerns about the publisher's intellectual reputation. In light of Sloterdijk's sudden influence over his protector, some journalists proclaimed the imminent marginalization of Habermas's intellectual voice and the confirmation of a trend that would see "the dilution of the rigor of the social sciences in cultural studies" and a confusion with lightweight literature focused only on "day-to-day problems, sketches of the present time and life-style sociology."[10] This presumed shift of knowledge toward triviality and of academic writing toward essays was, in the eyes of its opponents, closely linked to Sloterdijk's unwarranted position, which he owed to Unseld's good graces. In other words, the fact that this "pop-philosopher" could have moved so close to one of the nerve centers of the production and reproduction of the German intellectual field generated tensions and concerns about the brand name of legitimate philosophy and about the quality control of the objects, methods, and issues worthy of the publisher's intellectual catalogue. At the very least, in the debates in the fall of 1999, this advocacy and its impact were already poisoning the arena in which the controversy mentioned earlier would emerge. Yet, far from blocking Sloterdijk's ascension, this episode provided him with a new launchpad, for which he showed his gratitude to the provider. Although Unseld, who passed away in 2012, would never know whether he had made the right gamble, his protégé did not forget to dedicate *In the World Interior of Capital* to him: "In memoriam Siegfried Unseld."

The field of philosophy

In the eyes of his critics, Sloterdijk's sudden rise no doubt had the appearance of an illegitimate show of strength. From the sidelines of the professional research activities that he loathed, the newcomer displayed other kinds of cultural capital (literary success and media stardom) in securing a nodal position in the key issue of defining the intellectual field and its discursive conventions.[11] In positional terms, we can thus say that those who saw him as a target simultaneously attacked (1) the rise of an agent who until then had occupied a subaltern position; (2) the threat of change in the hierarchy of receivable capital in consecrated grounds; and, above all, (3) the reinstatement of authors and currents vilified by dominant, central positions and the removal of the firm grip the latter had long had over the former.

It is worth recalling in this regard that prior to the "Rules for the Human Zoo" controversy, the September 17, 1998, federal elections put an end to the 16-year rule of the Christian Democrats (CDU/CSU). Gerhard Schröder's Social Democratic Party won 44.5 percent of the seats in the Bundestag and formed an alliance with the Green Party, which gave them an absolute majority. This tidal change had a particular signification: for the first time, the Federal Republic of Germany would experience life under an administration born after the war. Chancellor Schröder (born in 1944) and the charismatic vice-chancellor from the Green Party, Joschka Fischer (born in 1948), incarnated the taking of power by a new generation. This red–green coalition lasted until 2005 and left its mark on political history. In terms of foreign affairs, it put an end to the traditional following of the herd by opposing the hawkish policy of the United States with regard to Iraq. With regard to domestic policy, the coalition symbolized the first years of the renaissance of Berlin as the capital city, which, in turn, served as a symbol for the renewal of an avowed desire to normalize the *Berliner Republik*. This said, this symbolic change would not be without victims.

Philosophy in Real Time: The 1999 "Eugenicist Posthumanism" Scandal

In July 1999, Sloterdijk gave a talk at Castle Elmau in Bavaria, the echoes of which would reverberate throughout Europe the following autumn. In "Rules for the Human Zoo," he put forward a dual thesis: the present day confirms the end of humanism in the arts (there has been a change of media . . .) and this contemporary situation requires us to re-read Heidegger, who, better than anyone else, had anticipated this crisis of humanism as the mode of production of human beings (. . . which requires us to rethink the means of domesticating humans). As a repetition of a talk given in Bale in June 1997, the Elmau talk provided an opportunity to reiterate these arguments at a conference dedicated to Martin Heidegger and Emmanuel Levinas, which had not foreshadowed anything particularly sensational.

However, among the journalists present at the conference, the *Frankfurter Rundschau*'s Martin Meggle produced a "report" that transposed the conference's erudite discussions onto a media and political terrain. In describing this interesting conference, which had taken place within the walls of a castle that had once belonged to a "Nazi sympathizer" and which was focused on the current relevance of a "Nazi thinker [Heidegger]," Meggle took direct aim at Sloterdijk. Since Sloterdijk had been obliged to reply to questions posed by the Israeli historian and Holocaust scholar Saul Friedländer to justify his examination of the horrors perpetrated in the name of humanism *after 1945*, Meggle's trenchant headline carried an air of scandal: "Real phantom and imaginary phantom. Peter Sloterdijk lectures Jewish thinkers about horror."[12] This sensationalist headline glossed over the nuances of the debate that arose in light of the Elmau conference and, as a result, forced Sloterdijk to publish his paper earlier than planned.[13]

Just what was so shocking about this talk? It was no doubt the provocative way in which Sloterdijk linked the obsolescence of literary humanism to the possible return of a form of eugenicism stripped of its former interdictions. He argued that we were witnessing eugenicism overlaid by biotechnology, which no longer functioned via "selection by anthology" – choosing beautiful domesticated literary works, as humanism put it – but, rather, by way of "breeding without breeder, an agentless biocultural drift" (RHZ 23). These arguments did not go unnoticed, particularly with regard to the fact that the specter of this selection – left to its own devices by a deleterious, decommissioned humanism – appeared to open the floodgates of Sloterdijk's imagination. He played on the entire gamut of possible ambiguities among nightmare, injunction, and opportunity by linking firm assertions with naive "questioning":

> It suffices for now to make clear that for the next period of time species politics will be decisive. That is, when it will be learned whether humanity (or at least its culturally decisive faction) will be able to achieve effective means of self-taming. A titanic battle is being waged in our contemporary culture between the civilizing and the bestializing impulses

and their associated media. Certainly, any great success in taming would be surprising in the face of an unparalleled wave of social developments that seems to be irresistibly eroding inhibitions. But whether this process will also eventuate in a genetic reform of the characteristics of the species; whether the present anthropotechnology portends an explicit future determination of traits; whether human beings as a species can transform birth fatalities into optimal births and prenatal selection – these are questions with which the evolutionary horizon, as always vague and risky, begins to glimmer. (RHZ 24)

Yet "Rules for the Human Zoo" does not go beyond the scope of these "questions." The provocation they engendered was likely due to the fact that they were expressed in a vitalist, biologizing vocabulary – human zoo, selection, taming, breeding, anthropotechnology, genetic reform – that was surely intended to strike a blow against the customs of humanist goodwill. The subtext of this provocative usage suggests that the right way of addressing the problem of education, the transmission of ideas and culture, is by a tradition other than humanism. In terms of form, however, "Sloterdijk had deliberately chosen the most terrifying topic and terms to violate the strongest taboo in German political culture."[14] It is for this reason that the real scandal had yet to emerge.

On September 2, 1999, Thomas Assheuer, editor of the weekly *Die Zeit*'s cultural pages, denounced Sloterdijk and his "Zarathustra project," in which he "coldly envisions the diabolic potential of genetic research."[15] Capitalizing on Assheuer's escalation of matters, in the September 6 edition of *Der Spiegel*, journalist Reinhard Mohr published an article with a title and a lead that also played on the diabolico-Nietzschean reference: "*Breeder of Overmen*. Philosopher Peter Sloterdijk advocates 'prenatal selection' and 'optional birth': Genetics as applied social critique. His most recent talk about 'human breeding' is akin to fascist rhetoric."[16] Mohr did not hesitate to quote selected passages of the talk even though Sloterdijk was still in the process of editing it for publication. Whatever changes Sloterdijk made were unimportant, Mohr wrote, because "we already know too much and too many audience members have already made a note of it." Absolved of responsibility by Assheuer's article, Mohr took up the accusation against this Zarathustra project, the genetic counterpart of the Manhattan project, and provided an overview of the phenomenon:

The Left's self-marginalization over the past few decades has led to a lustrous new relativism . . . It is thus no happenstance that Suhrkamp, the flagship of the leftist intelligentsia and its regent Siegfried Unseld, houses two eminent authors characterized by their decidedly antidemocratic, anti-Western and fascistico-totalitarian verve: Peter Sloterdijk and Peter Handke.[17]

Assheuer and Mohr's charge would bear fruit. Nennen's exhaustive study revealed that the storm generated by the *Die Zeit/Der Spiegel* tandem gave rise to pan-European reactions involving more than 600 articles and letters to the editor. In particular, this outpouring shows that the construction of the philosophical arena does not always obey strictly internal and autonomous criteria, but can stem from the organization of public discourse and the struggles to which it gives rise with regard to conventions to be respected or violated:

> The Sloterdijk debate is a conclusive example of the practice of social discourse. Throughout its development, we can study what a "discourse" really is and even identify its traces via the debate. To be sure, the real-time evolution of this discourse cannot be understood in relation to a rationalist ideal. Rather, it shows the extent to which the rules of the ideal conditions for a so-called theoretical model of rational discourse are unrealistic. What is viewed as scholarly by the community of scholars is rarely considered as such in a debate published in the *talk-of-the-town* section of newspapers or magazines, or in society.[18]

Sloterdijk would exploit this fault line between acknowledgment by academic peers and the forceful act by which the legitimacy of a philosophical discourse can earn its stripes by infiltrating social discourse. Indeed, he fully seized the opportunity and, under the watchful public eye, succeeded in redefining the terms of the debate by turning the insidiousness of these false accusations against the accusers.

The humiliation of Habermas

On September 9, 1999, *Die Zeit* published two letters to the editor by Sloterdijk. Collectively entitled "Critical Theory is Dead,"[19] the first of these letters was addressed to Thomas Assheuer. It replied briefly to his article by ironically congratulating him for having drawn public attention to extremely important philosophical questions of interest to a significant number of sociologists and scholars for several decades. It also thanked him for having dared to uncloister philosophy from its academic tower and to locate the debate in social discourse. However, it asked Assheuer to explain how he had gotten his hands on an unpublished paper and to show Sloterdijk this bootlegged version so that he could compare it to his own and correct some misinterpretations:

> I would gladly compare your version to mine to see whether we are using the same document. In my paper, for example, there is a passage in which I view the Nietzschean vision of breeding as hysterical and not appropriate for our times and in which I argue that the notion of the Overman (*Übermensch*) can no longer have any meaning for us.

This first letter provided a few other excerpts from the talk that contradicted the fallacious aspects of Assheuer's work and ended by deploring contemporary journalistic work – in which Assheuer excelled – that amounted to sounding the alarm for its own sake. Quoting himself, Sloterdijk noted that this was a characteristic of society that he had discussed elsewhere (SV 110–30), and he invited Assheuer to *read* his work.

The letter to Assheuer was followed by a second one addressed to Jürgen Habermas, who, however, had not uttered a single word in public about the ongoing debate:

> Dear Mister Habermas,
>   It is well known that rumors travel quickly. We have all one day or another seen how they travel as quickly as a malign spirit. As such, as the last link in this chain of whispers, I learned in a delayed manner, while I was on vacation in the south of France, that you felt it important to comment on Heidegger's *Letter on Humanism* via me and my Elmau talk. In doing so, you chose to use words from your polemical reservoir and your political vocabulary, in which the expression *young conservative* plays a large role.
>   Even though you and I have known calmer days, a friendship abandoned, and even though I do not wish to repress the affect of the memory of the high esteem I felt for you as the author of several monumental works both for me and for my generation, I am writing to you to comply, for my part, with the requirements of a return to a form of entente through non-defamatory dialogue. I am taking this first step even though the situation is such that it required you to do so. I respect the privilege of elders which you invoke in my case. And, for the time being, I view your omissions as simple mistakes that you can correct, and your judgments as expressions of a state that could find a more temperate form.

This initial invitation, in which the young philosopher acknowledged the privileged status owed to his elder counterpart, whom he pardoned for having momentarily derogated from the rules of orderly public debate, was followed by a simultaneously exasperated and supplicating demand for acknowledgement and for dialogue:

> I respectfully ask you to consider my expression *for the time being*. It expresses well the fact that I have almost reached the limits of my patience. You have, Mr Habermas, spoken *of* me to others on many occasions, but never *with* me. In a community that privileges argumentation, doing so is disturbing; coming from a theorist of democratic dialogue, it is nonsensical.

Although Sloterdijk was by no means taken in by the logic of polemic as the antithesis of serene communication, he attempted to elevate himself to the ranks of a legitimate interlocutor vis-à-vis Habermasian authority, of which he was more than free to demand communicational reciprocity. However, to ensure that things were not left at that, Sloterdijk followed up with two accusations that would assuredly force a reply:

> Between Hamburg and Jerusalem, you have often made telephone calls to convert others to your contempt. You have exercised undue pressure on colleagues who liked my Elmau talk. What is more, in contravention of the ethics of academic and public collegiality, you have produced bootlegged versions of the manuscript (which was given to you by the publisher for your private use) with the insidious purpose of sending them to journalists who are former students of yours, to whom you explicitly suggested the wrong interpretation and demanded that they take action. You proceeded by way of latent extortions by reproaching the attendees of the Elmau conference, whose reactions in situ to my talk were not as eccentric as yours. You called upon an editor at *Die Zeit* and a journalist at *Der Spiegel* to produce alarmist articles in which your name was not to appear. You first whispered in the ear of Assheuer, and then Mohr did his duty.

Theft, secret plot, and remote manipulation of the public space: Sloterdijk goes on at length about the nefarious consequences of the meta-scandal for the naive or superhuman pretensions – *too good to be true* – of communicative action that Habermas himself had circumvented:

> Should we now talk about your own turn (*Kehre*)? At the very least, we can now better understand what you and your docile disciples mean by the idea of discussion, of thought and taking charge of problems in public and sincerely. You have shown in an exemplary manner how you authorized the wrong reading as a battle weapon. You built a scene that helps us understand the way in which the dyslexia of brave disciples can serve the ends of your opportunism. Can we expect better of an Enlightenment thinker?

Lastly, taking advantage of this unprecedented opportunity to promote his work, the accused transformed himself into accuser and held up the meaning of the ongoing polemic for all to see. Transposing this exchange in generational terms, he argued that the time of the hyper-morality of the sons of the Nazi period was over and that this necessarily entailed a shift in the order of intellectual positions and schools of legitimate thought. Sloterdijk argued that we were witness to the death of the Frankfurt School, of which Habermas was the ultimate representative:

> Alas, dear Habermas, I say it quite willingly, it's over. The days of sons with good or bad consciences are over. What can be so sad about this?

It opens a new chapter. That which I wanted to philosophically contribute as a theorist of the human dream can be found in my latest two books [the first two volumes of *Spheres*].

On this day, September 2nd, critical theory is dead. The long-bedridden, morose old lady has now completely disappeared. We will meditate at her grave not only to take stock, but also to think about the end of an hypocrisy. To think (*Denken*) means to thank (*Danken*), said Heidegger. I would add that to think also means to breathe.

Yours respectfully, P. Sl.

If Heidegger opened critical theory's funeral cortege here, it was because Sloterdijk wanted to take advantage of the gap offered to him by Habermas to alter the convention of legitimate philosophical resources, the circulation of which the Frankfurt School had long wanted to police for the benefit of its own products. The meta-discussion that Sloterdijk wanted to engender thus went beyond the framework of the scandal caused by his Elmau talk: it was renewal in the way of philosophizing that was at issue, and Habermas was obliged to acknowledge that he was no longer able to legitimately inhibit it.

Following Sloterdijk's reply to Assheuer–Habermas, Suhrkamp was forced to speed up publication of the sulfurous manuscript. The entire document was put on line on the publisher's website and, because of massive downloading, continued to fuel the intellectual press. The polemic was now composed of several strata: the received or non-receivable version of Sloterdijk's talk; its use or misuse by the press; and the critique or the defense of critical theory within the framework of a generational dispute.

On September 16, Habermas came out of the shadows. He replied to Sloterdijk in the pages of *Die Zeit*. Entitled "Message from the Malign Spirit," Habermas's short letter attempted to refute the accusations levied against him. He attacked his accuser instead: "[Sloterdijk] is throwing sand in the eyes of the public when he defines himself as an inoffensive bio-ethicist."[20] He also wanted to deny the cabal argument: "Sloterdijk also invents an amusing story about spirits in which there is a big bad spirit and many small spirits at his service." To this end, Habermas developed a five-point commentary on the affair with a view to rectifying the "facts" (a commentary that would subsequently be contradicted): (1) he claimed to have learned about this matter in the newspapers and from what was said by certain irritated witnesses; (2) he denied once again any communication with anyone involved in *Die Zeit* and *Der Spiegel*'s offensive; (3) he stated that it was Sloterdijk's announcement of the upcoming publication of his talk that drew his interest to its contents and that as a close collaborator of Suhrkamp's academic program, he was worried that the publisher would step into a new political scandal; (4) he declared that his fears were confirmed after reading the *Der Spiegel* article by Mohr, a journalist he did not personally know and with whom he had never interceded; and (5) he stated that as an advocate of human rights, no one would be surprised to learn that he had exchanges with friends he had met over the years. Although Thomas Assheuer was part of this circle of friends, Habermas denied that Assheuer was his disciple.

Following these clarifications, Habermas added that he had never had the occasion until the present moment to discuss the Sloterdijk affair with his friends. "[Sloterdijk] is mistaken about my power of influence and, above all, he overestimates my interest in his work and the amount of time and energy I have invested in reading his manuscript." As such, he declined any invitation to have a dialogue with an "eventual peer." However, he conceded that perhaps this debate revealed a change in German intellectual dynamics, of which Sloterdijk was the recent symptom:

> Perhaps Sloterdijk really does incarnate something new on the *Berliner Republik* market. Perhaps the mentality of someone born in 1947, who claims, in 1999, to be able to freely choose his past meets a real demand by the new generation. In our case, the half-generation that separates us marks a difference in vision in this regard.

However, this "difference in vision" was not merely generational. In the case of the Sloterdijk affair, it was altogether factual. The cabal organized by Habermas was not something imagined by Sloterdijk. On the contrary, on September 23, the ARD television station's program *Tagesthemen* broadcast the contents of a faxed letter from Habermas to Assheuer in which Habermas leaked excerpts from the talk that he described as "genuinely fascistic."[21] Although the story went national, it was never commented on by Habermas, who, notwithstanding his own denials, had been caught out.[22]

Another Foreseeable Collision: The 2009 Dispute over Income Tax

A close disciple of Jürgen Habermas, Axel Honneth has been director of the Institute for Social Research in Frankfurt since 2001. In line with the famous school's multiple post-Marxist turns, he works on "the paradoxes of capitalist modernization," with particular emphasis on liberal issues such as justice, recognition, and exclusion in democratic regimes. Working in the shadow of his prestigious forerunners, Honneth has sought to preserve the moral heritage of critical theory, its intellectual vigilance, and its duty to defend the underprivileged, and these features distinctively marked his interventions during the 2009 controversy. In retrospect, however, it appears as though the

Honneth–Sloterdijk polemic had already been foreshadowed, if not predetermined, by the 1999 Habermas–Sloterdijk scandal.[23] Nevertheless, in less than a decade after this months-long public struggle, Sloterdijk had risen to the rank of an international philosopher, and this newfound position differed strikingly from his weaker status in 1999 when he fought with the Frankfurt School's former leading light. In the new sky over the *Berliner Republik*, most members of the post-World War II generation were pushing for a change of guard in all spheres of society, even if this meant breaking with the moral interdictions of their elders. In the acrimonious view of Honneth, this milieu represented by Sloterdijk was to be seen "as an elite which has read Michel Foucault and which, with the help of a free, elastic and acrobatic mental attitude, has been able to rapidly seize every power position."[24] Though the good old days of the Frankfurt School's pre-eminence really seemed to be over, Sloterdijk's ascension to a position of prominence represented more than just the outcome of an intergenerational conflict. Rather, it was the result of taking an unusual and ambitious path that enabled Sloterdijk to advocate an intellectual ethos that brought the usual prestige granted to the scholarly milieu into question.

To return to Honneth's remark on the "Foucauldian elite," these otherwise polemical and pejorative analyses were symptomatic of a broader feeling of resentment toward Sloterdijk on the part of the scholarly community. From the perspective of the self-appointed authoritative voices of academia, Sloterdijk's success was the result of a fraudulent *coup de force* by an author who had produced merely "minor" cultural capital (as a bestseller and media personality), and yet had nevertheless managed to threaten the ethos traditionally reserved to scholars. On the one hand, Sloterdijk proposed a thought experiment, a set of provocative propositions that "freely speculated" but that nevertheless sought to encourage a radical change in fiscal mentality. On the other hand, Honneth was bound to a philosophy of responsibility, a public-debate ethics that had to serve as the linchpin of the agora and defend analytical prudence as well as the intellectual's political and academic probity.

From grabbing hands to giving hands: a rendezvous *manqué*

"Today, we are not living 'in capitalism' – as thoughtless and hysterical rhetoric suggests over and over again – but in an order of things that should be defined *cum grano salis* as a mass-media-driven, tax-grabbing semi-socialism . . . Thus, the direct and selfish exploitation of the feudal era has been transformed in the modern age into a juridically constrained and almost disinterested state kleptocracy."[25] Such was the outrageous bombshell Sloterdijk threw at the consensus over the principles of the German welfare state. When questioned by the *Frankfurter*

Allgemeine Zeitung about the "future of capitalism," he chose to answer with this dark portrait of a state that stripped its most productive citizens by overtaxing them,[26] not for the sake of its social responsibilities (the public treasury could no longer afford it), but to accomplish a Proudhonist-Marxist program born out of a deep ressentiment against property and wealth.[27] "Expropriate the expropriator" had become, wrote Sloterdijk, "expropriation for expropriation's sake," and this ensured that nobody owned anything because "property is theft." Starting with a critical examination of these hateful theses against comfortable living, Sloterdijk adopted a position under the banner of a sort of Nietzschean prodigality, and suggested nothing less than an alternative taxation system that would rely on the noble ethics of giving hands (donations to the state in lieu of direct taxation) on the part of its most productive and wealthiest citizens: "This courageous turn would have to show that, in the eternal struggle between greed and magnanimity, the latter can sometimes win."[28]

Though clearly naive, this curious proposition was far from innocent. Sloterdijk purposely provoked German orthodoxy by playing all the notes of its scale. Indeed, a few months later, the progressive weekly *Die Zeit* published a strong reply from Honneth against Sloterdijk's unacceptable prescriptions, in which Honneth crudely denounced "the irresponsible thesis that has been thrown at the world's face with such nonchalance."[29] He immediately reiterated the convention by which the welfare state (in Germany, France, Great Britain, and elsewhere) had to be seen as "the result of the fierce struggle of the workers' movement," whose actors simply "demanded the equality in treatment that has been promised by the liberal constitution in democratic countries." No need here to refer to "greed, envy or ressentiment" to be able to understand the legitimate battle of these oppressed people "that only seek to actualize the moral principles of modern law." These factual and moral clarifications were delivered alongside a series of recriminations against *écriture automatique* à la Sloterdijk, a star who had not only become the darling of the media but who dangerously sought to serve now as a political advisor. In this regard, Honneth's comment is justified in that Sloterdijk admitted that these arguments were of considerable interest to the federal minister of finance, Wolfgang Schäuble, whom he was to meet in early 2010.[30] The gratuitousness of this philosophical exercise thus contained a realist political dimension that divided the German intelligentsia.

In his well-justified critique, Honneth was nevertheless cautious enough not to take a position on the issue of public debt. Nor did he comment on the numbers Sloterdijk referred to when he depicted "hyper-progressive" taxation as a system in which "the top 20% of taxpayers produce over 70% of the State's income,"[31] a fact he treated as a potential precursor to a "civil war over taxation." There was not even a single serious word on the "ethics of giving hands," Sloterdijk's core proposition: it seems that it was out of the question, from Honneth's standpoint, to let anyone be seduced by the tricks of this soothsayer. Yet in spite of this skepticism, if one truly lends oneself to the thought experiment proposed here, it might appear that the concept of donation was far more provocative than what Honneth dared to see in it; giving is certainly the great denial of the liberal vulgate and its egoistic subject (whose twin became the social democrat subject who *still* defines himself by lack and dissatisfaction even though he enjoys an opulent, privileged position). If socialist hatred toward property has been transformed into state kleptocracy, says Sloterdijk, one should first see in this movement the tragic incapacity to imagine humans as creatures capable of magnanimity. From the stance of forgotten aristocratic virtues (honor, pride, and prodigality), Sloterdijk argues that it is about time that prosperous people truly *give* instead of being *forced to give* in the name of a negative anthropology that multiplies the "envious" on the one hand and the "greedy" on the other. Why are we not able to give? Why does the state transform this presumed incapacity into a general principle? In an affirmative manner that would strip away the mask, the cultural turn advocated by Sloterdijk would have the Prodigal say: *I am wealthy, therefore I give*. This would then uncover the hypocritical shame of a life of ease (a material status now enjoyed by an unprecedentedly large number of people in Western countries) and help the Prodigals to acknowledge their objective plenitude, one that needs to be broadly shared.

Yet this was not exactly the bucolic field on which this new "philosophy of money" was received by the all-too-responsible position of Honneth and dozens of other left- or right-wing intellectuals (including Paul Kirchhof, a conservative jurist,[32] and Ulrich Beck, a sociologist[33]) who rejected Sloterdijk's proposition in public.[34] Among these critics, Honneth was by far the most eager to fight an "objective enemy" in a spirit of vengeance against the illegitimate ascension of this "intellectual decorated with the highest academic distinctions."[35] As if everything had been predetermined, *Die Zeit* immediately opened its pages to Sloterdijk to set the stage for a kind of second-rate repetition of the 1999 scandal. However, the sought-after collision did not take place. While refusing the fight in a letter published in the *Frankfurter Allgemeine Zeitung*, Sloterdijk denigrated the terms of this fake controversy and mocked the accusation of his challenger: "If our nervous philosophy professor is incapable and unwilling to fairly apprehend a twelve-page essay, without rough distortions and without turning the argument on its head, then it makes no sense in advance to speak with him about the difference between our respective 'modes of philosophizing'."[36] Sloterdijk also complained about the fact that Honneth had merely stitched together a sheer fabric of "last-minute quotations" that betrayed not only his "eight-thousand-page delay" but also his incapacity to comment on the work with any competence.

This exchange of ad hominem salvoes undoubtedly undermined the birth of a debate. Ten years after his prolonged, though modestly successful skirmish with Habermas, Sloterdijk showed that there was no reason for him to enter into a dialogue with the Frankfurt School to consolidate his position. Furthermore, he dared to posit an asymmetrical relationship between himself and the declining school. Nevertheless, and despite the fact that the Sloterdijk–Honneth Affair did not take place as planned, the German press begged for some additional comments and analyses from both sides. For his part, Honneth confessed that he still favored "the real protection of equality of opportunities" even though he acknowledged that this mission "[could] no longer be under the responsibility of the old welfare state program, which has lost its basis through demographic and economic changes in the last few decades."[37] Sloterdijk, on the other hand, proposed a manifesto against the spirit of "lack and need" that paralyzed Germany, in which he exhorted his fellow citizens to face the unprecedented state of luxury that now characterized Western standards: "The truth indeed is that we can no longer be understood, and have not been in a position to be understood for some time, by most other cultures on Earth."[38] Acting both as the prince's advisor and as naive speculative philosopher, Sloterdijk also wanted to anchor his political proposition in his broader diagnoses, found in the works that Honneth et al. did not dare to take into account: "I start from an anthropological stance where humans are seen as being more than greedy grabbers. They have to be considered as giving-beings as well as taking-beings."[39] Yet there remains the question of how this argument can shed light on a generally misunderstood (if not misleading) proposition. Given that chapter 5 will focus more closely on this issue of an "ethic of giving," let us turn our attention here to the political, if not partisan effects of these well-calculated moves by someone who said that he was no longer apolitical, and as such, like the astrologer gazing up at the stars in Aesop's fable, risked falling into wells.

From Nightingale to Hawk

Sloterdijk's proposals about "voluntary income tax" are not among the most interesting or stimulating in his writings, and could well figure among the few "sterile seeds" in a much broader "literary sowing of the fields."[40] However, it would be an error to isolate them from his more profound works, in that this manifesto in favor of achievers is the fiscal counterpart of the pride (see chapter 1) and ascetic verticality (see chapter 2) at the heart of his concerns and prescriptions in the first decade of the 2000s. In the years following 9/11, Sloterdijk was less of a nightingale that bothered clerics, politicians, and conformists from a distance. Rather, he participated in a realistic turn that has imbued the ambient air breathed by all Western elites since 2001. To be sure, while there is something of an objective exaggeration in the fact of portraying Sloterdijk as a hawk,[41] it is nevertheless a plausible avenue given that what his critics or adversaries had intuitively identified as a hawkish turn (*Kehre*) in *Rage and Time* was confirmed in subsequent years. As someone who was worried about the drawbacks of peace and idleness, he was less of an Epicurean than a Stoic,[42] less of a philosopher dog than a mouthpiece for the economic elite and productivist norm. Indeed, in his notes for himself in the week preceding the start of the "giving hands" scandal, he had already begun to rage against the idea of a guaranteed minimum income, which, in his view, would make indolence an "existential norm":

> This claim has always struck me as more symbolic than practical because it has already been effectively met through a series of guaranteed measures . . . The anthropology of a minimum income raises the triad consisting of the unemployed, prisoners and bohemians to the rank of an existential norm in the Western world. One can note in these claims a certain laudable tolerance: for those who want to earn more and to indulge themselves more, we acknowledge the right to provide for the society of the provided. In *Falconer*, Cheever's novel about prisons, we can see what a society of this kind will come to: basic supplies, then methadone or bread and illusions. (ZT 214–15)

This final section will examine Sloterdijk's politicization and his possible metamorphosis into a falconer no longer satisfied with being a shrewd observer of the zeitgeist and who wants to be an agent of transformation of the vocabulary of social democracy. The income tax dispute was not only a summit of Sloterdijk's political involvement; it distanced him from his first writings about the idealization of the demobilized dropout and the happiness of those who have nothing to do (see chapter 1).

What does it mean to be a social democrat today?

"For family and personal reasons, and not necessarily philosophical ones, I have *never* been able to vote for anything other than the Social Democratic Party of Germany."[43] In mid-controversy, this confession by Sloterdijk was intended to nuance his position with regard to the electoral collapse of the party, which saw itself returned to the ranks of the opposition in 2009. But what does it mean to be a social democrat in light of the regimes of Tony Blair, Lionel Jospin, and Gerhard Schröder?[44] Were these not already political parties that had struck the overthrow of capitalism from their program and had aligned themselves with the insurmountable imperatives of the market economy? Were they not all convinced that growth and productivity had become the norms for the center-left?[45]

However, Sloterdijk appeared to want more than Blairism for German social democracy. At many moments during the scandal, it was, rather, the American dream of "generalized philanthropy" that served as a source of inspiration:

> Americans do not believe that success engenders a debt. The image of the individual upon which their political culture is based leaves considerable room for the generous dimension of social behaviour. As such, the donor dimension among citizens is systematically encouraged. We, too, in Germany and Europe, would be well advised to become a civilization of competition in giving.[46]

More precisely, this ideal is based on the fear that Sloterdijk revealed afterwards in his long, post-controversy epilogue, namely that there would be an exodus of productive individuals from Germany: "Among the 650,000 people who bid adieu to Germany every year, 150,000 of them are highly qualified. They are thus lost to the national labour market and for the moment no immigration of the same sort replaces them."[47] Moreover, in this aging country, it is young people and "smart" people who are massively opting to leave and settle in anglophone countries. The signs of a hawkish political mood are accumulating: against indolence, against the exodus of achievers, against a strong fiscal state, etc. By crossing this mood with the one infusing *Reflections of a Not Anymore Unpolitical* (RNU 48), this appeal to the American model and the fear of a European decline overlap the dichotomy between a society of entertainment (erotic pole) and a society ready for war (thymotic pole), which has visibly become a permanent analytic framework since the publication of *Rage and Time* and the politico-physiological overthrow discussed in chapter 1.

In the shorter term, Sloterdijk wanted to link his analyses to the immediate results of Germany's 2009 federal elections. Indeed, all the conclusions of Sloterdijk's manifesto in defense of society's achievers transform his philosophical insights into a veritable meteor shower of ideological advice addressed to Germany's main political parties. Growing tired of the "red–green" and "red–black" coalitions, Sloterdijk was delighted with the rise of the "yellows" (the color of the Liberal party), who, by reaching their highest historical summit of 93 seats in the Bundestag in September 2009, had been able to participate in the new "yellow–black" coalition. As if he had been preparing his own expedition to Syracuse,[48] Sloterdijk took advantage of this new parliamentary context by advocating a long series of recommendations and prognostics. The victory of the blacks and yellows (conservatives and liberals) was seen here not only as the new political expression of the nation's overachievers, but also as a huge challenge for the reds (social democrats). In order to continue winning battles for the cause of the unprivileged and oppressed, the German left would now have to make its appeals "first and foremost to the hard core of society's top producers and only secondarily to the unemployed they seek to help in the first place."[49]

Noblesse oblige?

Sloterdijk's friendly prescriptions advocating the awakening of a "thymotic left" are aligned with his fears (exodus of young people and implementation of a norm of indolence) and the frighteningly concrete meaning that he wishes to give to the figure of the vertical, ascetic, high-performance, and athletic individual.[50] However, this current coherence between his theory and politics conceals a rupture with his writings on the cynicism of the ruling class and infinite mobilization. Against the "spirit of gravity" (which can also easily be associated with the paralysis of indolence, with the weight of fiscal obligations, or simply with the idea of equality), since the publication of *You Must Change Your Life* Sloterdijk has clearly committed himself as in favor of heroic performance that escapes this base-camp culture. He leaves the oriental plains to think from atop the occidental summits. In doing so, he not only appears to be "closer to the Stoics than to the Cynics,"[51] but also walks the very thin line of irony that changes sides from critique that unmasks to critique that protects, that is, from kynicism to cynicism.

In this regard, neither the kynics nor Diogenes appear in this book on the virtues of exercise, which settles for a few allusions to Cynics in general (MCL 195, 409, 490). Yet Diogenes' "performance" athletically targets the autarchy of those who do not participate in the powers that harness the simple fact of living. "His spectacular poverty is the price of freedom" (CCR 158) and is not to be confused with miserabilism. Rather, it incarnates a very frugal idea of pride. What would Diogenes have said while strolling about with his lantern among the disciplined ranks of overachievers who gaze at themselves in the mirrors of their overcrowded fitness rooms? Discouraged by the gravitational force of the welfare state that steals from them, do these smart young people have some idea of the rigors of freedom? And what can we say about these other smart young people who do not want to lose their life by earning it – those who work less to travel more, who explore new paths in the sharing of (gendered) housework, and who demand both fair pay for the shameful and horizontal tasks associated with care work and that the state and capital accord them the right to spend more time with their children? Does this indolence stem from an acute awareness that life is short, at a time when the dreams of the comfortably retired are going up in smoke in the stock market, and are hugely corrected by the obligatory lengthening of working life to obtain increasingly smaller pensions?

For the moment, there are no clear answers to these questions within Sloterdijk's wide philosophical scope. While we might be tempted to move him closer to the Stoics, we still have to clarify his whereabouts. Between the depressed Marcus Aurelius, irritated by humans and politics, and the sacrificial engagement of Cicero, distrustful of dropouts from citizenship, there is still the view from below of the slave Epictetus, who dominates his body, and the view from above of Seneca, who laughs at shipwrecks from afar. While the filters have yet to be applied to the Instagram snapshot of political life, we can certainly hear in Sloterdijk's chortling about the reverses of social democracy or the demands for a guaranteed minimum income the echo of Lucian the Mocker's laughter (see chapter 1, note 24) as he looks away from critique from below to comfort the powerful in their certitudes: "The cynical master lifts the mask, smiles at his weak adversary, and suppresses him. *C'est la vie. Noblesse oblige.* Order must prevail" (CCR 111).

In realpolitik, political philosophers tend to be either unredeemable or naive. As such, we have to temper our judgment not only on the effects Sloterdijk could have on social democracy but on the nature of the skillfully coded messages in the trial balloons that he releases with a false nonchalance and perhaps with no evil intentions. Although it is not yet possible to definitively measure this politicization, we can still examine Nietzsche's influence on this shift. The thinker who was sick with agony upon hearing the rumor that dirty workers had set fire to the Louvre in 1871 was the same thinker who wrote some of the most damning words about the idea of democratic equality.[52] It might be possible to read Nietzsche with scissors in hand and take from him only what appears to be compatible with democratic culture by rendering him politically inoffensive. For one of his severe critics, however, doing so would be in vain because Nietzsche "must be viewed, rather, as a *totus politicus*."[53] The least we can say is that he is in no way compatible with equality because his critique of the ressentiment of the weak is always accompanied by that of the compassion of the strong.

> Not only is there nothing noble about ressentiment and compassion, but they are also particularly pernicious: they are constitutive of two moments, from below and from above, of the crisis of culture. The end result of historical and psychological inquiry into moral sentiments is the moral decapitation of the slave revolt: the social question about which so much is said is only the inconvenient guilt of the lucky on the part of life's losers who, in gargling inflated ideals and words, do nothing more than give free reign to the instinct for vengeance.[54]

On the theoretical philosophical level, Sloterdijk skillfully tacks between the promises of and limits to the uses of Nietzsche (who clearly dominates all of his writings) in democratic culture. Politics sometimes obeys another mechanism than philosophical euphemization and does not allow for as tight a control of the message. Pride, verticality, performance asceticism, income tax, and giving: each has its own particular ideological resonance, and while Sloterdijk's plastic power over language is incontestable, the reception of his discourse as ideology can only elude him, especially when he makes it a virtue to ignore strategic issues and the astronomy of a given conjuncture, even though it might mean falling into wells. One of the signs that the planets move quickly through the skies over Berlin is that Sloterdijk's brief Platonic idyll with the Liberal Party has already come to an end because of the collapse of its electoral support in 2013, which led to the loss of all the 93 seats it had won in 2009. The Germany of overachievers is gently drifting toward a quiet return to Kohl, with a third term obtained by Merkel and the conservatives.

5

Therapy

"We should have become a sun but have become a savings account instead" (ZT 417). Although we can criticize his recent political views and note that the aging Sloterdijk has left many of the ideas of his insolent youth by the wayside, he remains a grand master of language. Be it the evocative power of his metaphors, the arresting, mirthful titles of his texts, or his razor-sharp sarcastic swipes that lift off the most sophisticated wigs of right-minded society to reveal what is hiding underneath, he convinces less by his rigor than by the pleasure he procures for his readers. This immediate and undeniable effect initially wins out over the cool assessment of second thoughts. One must measure up to this redoubtable prose when entering into a debate with this master. He feels by no means constrained by any of academia's generally accepted rules: self-censure, minimization of declarations, occupation of a position in the intellectual field, a careerist strategy, sham alliances, debates without debate, and recanting one's own words.

This last chapter provides an impressionistic portrait of Sloterdijk's panoply of therapeutic prescriptions. It retrospectively explores the way in which his philosophical project is filled with "piece[s] of exemplary healing" (CCR xxxvi). This pharmakon for an alter-modernity oscillates between a re-enactment of Epicurean withdrawal that recreates the enclosure of a healthy, sustainable microcity, on the one hand, and the virtues of strong belonging that undermines the supremacy of bourgeois, bellicose, and greedy subjectivity, on the other. This general therapy prescribes a series of alternative exercises that constitute an intellectual hygiene that can be broken down into five pharmaka: extra-university garden, grotesque humor, the poetics of disarmament, ecstatic proximity, and solar language.

The Karlsruhe Garden

Sloterdijk's very recognizable and unique independence and style in the intellectual world are due to a few exploits and his improbable occupation of an exceptional position as a professional thinker. It is worth recalling here that Sloterdijk is an author of philosophical best-sellers and not accountable to a faculty dean. Although this does not explain everything, it does put us on the trail of a rare case in an age of overspecialization in the scholarly industry. This rarity is less a novel occurrence than the improbable persistence of an old intellectual model. By analogy, we can link Sloterdijk's status to that of the gentlemen who characterized the early days of modernity:

> [F]rom the birth of Francis Bacon in 1561 to the death of David Hume in 1776 . . . not one first-rate philosophic mind in Europe is permanently associated with a university . . . The philosophers in the age of the gentleman are not so much at the centers of civilization as at its periphery – not like Plato in Athens or Saint Thomas at Paris and the papal court, but rather in small villages, obscure townships, or on country estates. And their work, for all its epistemological persuasiveness, has the quality of philosophy by men in retreat.[1]

The virtues of intellectuals in Epicurean retreat are the source of the irreverent successes of modern philosophy, which in its early days could develop only outside the institutional walls of the *universitas*. During this period, personal wealth, patronage, sponsorship, and the book market offered exceptionally propitious conditions for extra-university intellectual activity. However, intellectual autonomy was both tenuous and conditional because it was susceptible to political whim, to the fragility of partisan or personal allegiances, or to the vicissitudes of general circumstances. "[This] did not encourage intellectuals to pursue autonomous concerns on a high level of abstraction; the attraction was toward partisan polemic, literary style, and topical public issues."[2] Nonetheless, this patronage market certainly enabled greater intellectual freedom than the traditional university. It was for this reason that progressive Enlightenment intellectuals viewed universities as outmoded, which led to the widespread idea that they should be abolished in favor of a system of major professional schools.

Sloterdijk undeniably incarnates a kind of resurrection or persistence of this model. As rector of the Karlsruhe University of Arts and Design, he himself works within this kind of professional school. This distance from the habitus of academic philosophy recalls the epic battles between schools and universities before the latter came to prevail as the dominant model. To be sure, the philosopher-rector

Sloterdijk benefits from a latitude and theoretical transversality that assuredly set him apart from the tone, the specialization, and the constraints that characterize innumerable campuses awash with subdued professors. To the extent that new ideas often stem from marginal spaces that succeed in supporting the independence of a small enclosed city within a larger city, the Karlsruhe garden appears to want to play on the formulas and postures of this rivalry between the co-opted university and the free school.

In Sloterdijk's mind, there is no doubt that contemporary universities provide little room for academic freedom. It is for this reason that he continually puts forward the idea of a non-university site for independent study. He defines an ideal type of school for a demobilizing theory of withdrawal in which initially there is "nothing to do":

> The critique of political kinetics will be the working title for studies undertaken in a transfaculty, post-university *Hochschule*. It could begin its activities wherever it is important to question systemic human movements to determine whether they are grounded. Like all previous university institutions, the transfaculty in which the awareness of movement is taught needs neutral spaces to which access is denied to the executive body and representatives of mobilizers – which represents the best tradition of protecting theory since the High Middle Ages in Europe. However, because nearly all the world's present-day universities have become prep schools for mobilization and cognitive subcontractors for the "attack of the present against all other ages," the critique of political kinetics must search for other spaces to carry out its studies. (ET 73)

The early formulation of this program – colored by scattered caustic remarks about the atrophy of super-specialization or the responsibility of professors who, because of their overly ordered lives, find themselves participating in closing their humanities faculties – returns to the fore whenever Sloterdijk notes that the appropriate angle of approach to current problems requires researchers to remove themselves from the world of scholars. Indeed, he advocates this exile when he reworks anthropotechnics (see chapter 2) in favor of a general disciplinics that "would require a suitably contemporary transformation of universities . . . [that] can only take place through a direct participation in the disciplines. Establishing an academic system with discipline-based content and methods would at once be the only realistic way to counteract the atrophy of the educational system, founded on a reformed idea of the subjects and tasks of a Great House of Knowledge" (MCL 156). This first cure requires us to think both elsewhere and differently. The master practices what he preaches here by setting an unlikely example.

Humor, Romantic Wit, and Grotesque Degradation

Sloterdijk's professional affiliation gives only a slight idea of his stylistic coordinates. This style's permissiveness and expressiveness have much deeper and older roots. Chapter 1 briefly presented the therapeutic promises of the centauric art of writing – the melding of art and philosophy – that Sloterdijk offers up as an antidote to the decline of the Enlightenment. Moreover, there is no field of creativity or artistic theory (music, architecture, painting, poetry, and opera) that escapes Sloterdijk's attention.[3] This aesthetic impulse dates from as a far back as the early writings of the German Romantics, who also favored art and literature as vehicles for escaping the domestication of thought. This claim for Romanticism might seem surprising. However, as Peter Weibel notes, even if the old debate between Enlightenment and Romanticism has changed since the early nineteenth century, moderns are still inextricably bound to their Romantic heritage:

> The quarrel between the Enlightenment and absolutism, between the concepts and intuition, between sensualism and spirituality, between rationality and religion, is clearly not over. It persists under other names and other conditions. Yet even though the old equations and calculations no longer hold, Moderns have to come to terms with the Romantic side. Sloterdijk's writing offers some possible avenues to this end.[4]

Sloterdijk opens up an important breach that allows us to think beyond the fixity of this debate by promoting some of the most relevant and penetrating aspects of the Romantic movement while simultaneously rejecting its tendency to reify the categories of nation, culture, church, and the like. Indeed, Sloterdijk likes to believe that he could be viewed as a "late Romantic with surplus graphomaniacal motors" (ZT 616). However, it can be no more than a post-Romantic school that breaks with all reactionary, outmoded, and organicist forms. Sloterdijk remains most faithful to Romanticism in his characteristic flashes of wit, manifested in his use of humor and grotesque degradation to save thought from foundering on seriousness and bodilessness.

A post-Romantic school

Early German Romanticism explored a form of thought that contested a serious-minded spirit that appeared to be on its way to prevailing within the walls of the university and to being monopolized by professional thinkers. In opposition to the Enlightenment, this small circle of resistance advocated the practice of a vernacular, inherently poetic Romantic science, also referred to as *Naturphilosophie*.[5] Poeticized science was a recurring theme in early Romanticism: "If you want to penetrate the heart of physics, then consecrate yourself to the mysteries of poetry."[6]

Novalis (1772–1801) and Friedrich Schlegel (1772–1829) were the main leaders of the Romantic, bohemian literary circle in Jena organized around the literary magazine *Athenaeum* (1798–1800). As translators of the canons venerated by the circle (Dante, Cervantes, and Shakespeare), the young Romantics called for a new form of aphoristic writing conceived as a new way of grasping the world with recourse to systems that betray the world. To grasp the world in a new light, it needs to be Romanticized and philosophy, science, and art must be brought together. The Romantic rebellion was opposed to bourgeois subjectivity and abstract universalism, and organized around two main theoretical and intellectual articulations that would lead it in two distinct directions: the first of which was cultural, bohemian, and experimental in nature, and the other political, authoritarian, and realistic. The former experienced a rich follow-up and reappropriation, which, via Schlegelian impulses, would be taken up by Heine and Nietzsche. Under Adam Müller's (1779–1829) doctrinaire development, the latter direction would not last beyond 1830, the moment at which the tense idealization of the Middle Ages found no transmission point in the great century of the German university. However, the bad reputation of conservative Romanticism was a fait accompli and overshadowed the aesthetic quests of its early moments: "After 1800, the trend for thinking in collective terms seized the Romantics . . . the Romantic metaphysics of the infinite became the metaphysics of history and society, of the mind of the people and the nation, and which would always make it harder for the *one* to extricate itself from the *us*."[7]

Prior to this conservative co-optation, which was helped along by the aging movement, the *Athenaeum*'s young Romanticism was, on the contrary, infused with a Dionysian spirit of subversion of bourgeois subjectivity. As Keith Ansell-Pearson notes, "[o]nce we open up intellectual inquiry to a Dionysian cosmology, we enter the epoch of the decentring of the subject and bid a respectful adieu to the fiction of autonomy."[8] This ethical/aesthetic rebellion sought in particular to abolish the boundaries between literature and life, and between art and existence, through the use of irony and wit in all expressive forms that foiled the spirit of the system. For Sloterdijk, "[if] literature were just literature and life just life, it would be impossible to make connections between the problems of literature and those of life . . . In the final analysis, a strict demarcation between literature and life can not be made so easily" (ZWK 35–6).[9] More profoundly, Romantic aestheticism was a positive response to the crisis of the Enlightenment that, via Kant, led to a negative conception of the use of critical reason. To sidestep the dilemma of opposing reason and the absolute, the Romantic response was to adopt an artistic posture:

> Their middle path between this dilemma was their aestheticism. They believed that art, and art alone, could fill the vacuum left by reason. If reason is essentially a negative power, art is basically a positive one. While reason can only criticize, art can create. For the instrument of art is the imagination, which has the power to produce an entire world. The romantics built upon one of Kant's and Fichte's fundamental insights: that we live in a world that we create; they add to it only that our creation should be a work of art. That is the sum and substance of their famous "magical idealism."[10]

This magic, bohemian circle secretly wanted to grow large enough to constitute a worldwide avant-garde of artists. This vision never came about. Novalis took his own life in 1801 and Schlegel withered following his conversion to conservative Catholicism. The *Athenaeum*'s reckless gestures remained so many bottles thrown into the ocean, a few fragments or literary sowings of fields that would have to await the arrival of a more fertile spirit.

This Romantic power – power of life, power of nature, power of art – found its greatest transmission point in the life and work of Nietzsche.[11] The orgiastic Dionysian genius of Greek culture in antiquity that he once identified in Wagner's *Gesamtkunstwerk* (ideal or total work of art) helped Nietzsche forge the weapons for his later radical critique of civilization, which he viewed as a physician would his or her patient. Through a rearticulation of early Romanticism, freed of its early influences, he reached a new level of autonomy and creativity in his own right. It is at this point in the narrative of the transmission of Romantic creativity that Sloterdijk's sketch of Nietzsche begins to take on the air of a self-portrait and marvellously reveals his own relationship to the Romanticism of the nightingales (see chapter 1): "Nietzsche made use of the romantic capability for looking back from the rationality of the day into the reason of the night in order to scout out, in his own way, the Dionysian energetics of the foundation of being" (TS 26).

Recently retired, errant voyager, and self-publisher, Nietzsche spent his energy on writing up until 1889: "he succeeded, albeit at a high price, in being an artist *as* scholar-scientist and a scholar-scientist *as* artist" (TS 12). In his essay on Nietzsche, Sloterdijk identifies *The Birth of Tragedy* as an attempt to revive the Romantic art of writing, and one for which Nietzsche would pay the professional price entailed by this revolt:

> For whatever the combination of sources and prototypes, the decisive element in it was centauric birth, that is, the setting loose of an infinitely consequential artistic and philosophical double-natured eloquence

within which Nietzsche's powers were bound together effectively for the first time. (TS 10)

But there is much more. Sloterdijk views this centauric tradition as the site of a revolution that seeks to deprofessionalize the exercise of thought in the century of professorial idealism. Far from being "unclassifiable," this art of writing extended the scope of Nietzsche's curiosity to include all fields of knowledge. It also engaged in multiple post-Romantic reappropriations for which he clearly served as a crucial transmission point at a time when the nineteenth and twentieth centuries appeared to be on the way to resembling one another. In a playful or perhaps strategic manner, Sloterdijk gathers together a few major names under the banner of this label reserved for "free spirits":

> From E.T.A. Hoffmann to Sigmund Freud, from Sören Kierkegaard to Theodore W. Adorno, from Novalis to Robert Musil, from Heinrich Heine to Alexander Kluge, from Paul Valéry to Octavio Paz, from Bertolt Brecht to Michel Foucault, and from Walter Benjamin to Roland Barthes – in each instance, the most communicative minds have presented themselves as temperaments and variations of the centauric genius. (TS 13)

To be sure, this "clique" says less about the sociological sources of the post-Romantic contagion than about the literary and philosophical figures privileged and admired by Sloterdijk (a partial list of whom includes Hoffmann, Kierkegaard, Novalis, and Nietzsche, four leading figures related to early Romanticism). The fact that he speaks about philosophical dispositions is equally revealing of this centauric genius's other requirement:[12] abolishing the boundary between life and art is tantamount to abolishing the boundary between body and mind. It is when he grapples with the bodies of philosophers that he makes us laugh the most. Indeed, it is during these insolent moments that Sloterdijk reminds his sympathetic readers that there is always an element of *eros* in scholarly material: the wave that can wash over the bodies of those who are seduced by philosophical laughter.

Grotesque humor

The young Sloterdijk (kynical and Dionysian) favored a plebeian lowering of philosophical respectability. This belittlement used the vulgar, the savage, the irreverent, and the grotesque to ridicule minds without bodies. As a viewpoint looking up from below, the plebeian critique of canonical sources corresponds to a subaltern position (on the margin of legitimate thought) and to thought constructed on themes traditionally viewed as subaltern (the vulgar materiality of thought and the base reality of the body). This duel between high and low even finds its grounding in Sloterdijk's satirical phenomenology of the human body (see CCR 139–54), in which he suggests that if our ass could have a conversation with our head, it would undoubtedly say: "I find that our relationship is shitty" (CCR 148).

In using humiliation via the body, Sloterdijk modernizes the idea that the body is the material and arena of truth for thought, found in both Diogenes and Nietzsche. Like them, Sloterdijk resorts to this satiric device to submit pure mind to the authority of its body to critique the limits and errors of professionals of rationality.

In inflicting wounds on the narcissism of its victim, laughing at respectability is not merely a footnote on a page of the book relating the birth of theory. In his study of popular culture in the Middle Ages, Mikhail Bakhtin argues that this laughter was a weapon constantly wielded by grotesque realism: "As such it is opposed to severance from the material and bodily roots of the world; it makes no pretence to renunciation of the earthy, or independence of the earth and the body."[13] Contra the universality of ideas, grotesque realism brandishes the claim that only instances of the earth and the body are referents that can be universalized. As such, grotesque realism's decisive weapon is degradation: "to concern oneself with the lower stratum of the body, the life of the belly and the reproductive organs; it therefore relates to acts of defecation and copulation, conception, pregnancy, and birth."[14] As a recurring aspect of the plebeian critique of dualism, this medieval genesis of grotesque realism – parody and desecration – is the heir to the kynical refusal of social schizophrenia (see chapter 1). From Diogenes to Eulenspiegel, from Heine to Arendt, and from Chaplin to Derrida, insolence and, even more, Jewish insolence are, in Sloterdijk's view, so many models of resistance to the hypocrisy and cynicism of parvenus.

Among the famous examples of this grotesque device, Sloterdijk singles out a sixteenth-century engraving representing an apocryphal scene in which the philosopher Aristotle, madly in love with Alexander the Great's mistress Phyllis, agreed to let her ride him like a horse and to submit to her every whim (CCR 254–6). Moreover, there are many pictorial and sculptural representations of Aristotle's humiliation, inspired by the French medieval poem *Lai d'Aristote*. In Sloterdijk's reading of this tale, this grotesque depiction shows how beauty's lash can subdue and humiliate wisdom and that a plebeian women can teach a philosopher a lesson because of his sexual dependence. Indeed, this very earthy dependence reveals that Aristotle's contemplative autarchy is without substance. Drawing on this kynical-feminist device, Sloterdijk critically analyzes phallic philosophy's obsession with conjuring up "dangerous vaginas" that pose a "permanent threat" to its bodily disposition, which has traditionally been described as inappropriate feminization.

In the same vein, in the third volume of *Spheres*, Sloterdijk ridicules the sages featured in Plato's *Laws* who discuss the remaking of the world while sitting atop a mountain following a flood. He is astonished to note that these "sodomitic, solitary shepherds" (SIII 267) excluded women and that the issue of gender was left in the background, "as if there was a tacit agreement among enlightened Greeks about the understanding we have of the transformation of alpine sodomy into urban pederasty, as long as the rest of their relations provide the State with its new citizens" (SIII 267). The prescient beautiful mind did not feel it necessary to include those who – with the exception of the euphemized procreation between and among "minds" – demand the right of maternity over the very discussion of this gathering of men.

Examples and anecdotes of this kind fill the pages of Sloterdijk's texts. Recall here the heckling in 1969 experienced by Adorno in his last classes from members of a women's collective who brandished their naked bodies against the disincarnated emancipation of the Frankfurt School master (see chapter 1). The critique is invariably the same: thought that evacuates the body will respond to its falseness by humiliation. For our part, the centerpiece of this humor of the grotesque is the special place Sloterdijk reserves for the "ass" in his psychosomatics of cynical reason. Between some thoughts on breasts and an exegesis on farts, the philosopher of the obscure well merits a long quote:

> The arse seems doomed to spend its life in the dark, as the beggar among body parts. It is the real idiot of the family. However, it would be a wonder if this black sheep of the body did not have its own opinion about everything that takes place in higher regions, similar to the declassed who often cast the most sober gaze on people in higher strata.
>
> ... The arse is the plebeian, the grass-roots democrat, and the cosmopolitan among the part of the body – in a word, the elementary kynical organ. It provides the solid material basis. It is at home on toilets all over the world. The International of Arses is the only worldwide organization that has no statutes, ideology, or dues. Its solidarity cannot be shaken. The arse crosses all borders playfully, unlike the head, to which borders and possessions mean a lot ... The proclivity for the elementary and the fundamental predisposes the arse especially to philosophy ... As representative of the kynical principle per se (able to survive anywhere, reduction to the essentials), the arse can hardly be brought under government control, although it cannot be denied that many an arsehole has given off nationalistic tones.
>
> Often beaten, kicked, and pinched, the arse has a worldview from below: plebeian, popular, realistic. Millennia of bad treatment have not passed over it without leaving a mark. They have trained it to be a materialist, albeit one with a dialectical tendency, which assumes that things are shitty but not hopeless.

. . . To understand the arse would be therefore the best preparatory study for philosophy, the somatic propaedeutic. How many constipated theories we would be spared! (CCR 147–50)

Obviously, a rapprochement between mind and body goes against the philosophical tradition extending from Socrates to Hegel. In his search for psychosomatic materialism and an "embodied intellect" (TS 50), the young Sloterdijk combined Dionysus (music and tragedy), Diogenes (bodily animality), and Nietzsche (centauric art of writing) to stem the decline of thought begun by Socrates, "the unmusical barbarian" (TS 57). This undertaking is inspired by a reading of Nietzsche that tends to exaggerate the importance of the Dionysian element of Greek culture. Ansell-Pearson suggests that the Greeks were the inventors not so much of materialism as of idealist discipline and asceticism, something Nietzsche knew full well: "What the Greeks achieve for Nietzsche is a more exalted possibility of human existence, one that never ceases to be human, and it is these 'possibilities' that continue to interest him in his later work."[15] The aging Sloterdijk comes back to this vertical idealism, which he also identifies with Nietzsche and which prescribes the exploration of these "possibilities" via ascetic or thymotic discipline, and not merely by way of the authority of the body (see chapter 2).

The Poetics of Disarmament

Whereas Nietzsche called for the capacity to ruminate, Sloterdijk prescribed the capacity for breathing: "The modern world process led to a point beyond which the most external path, politics, and the most inner path, meditation, speak the same language; both revolve around the principle that only a '*relaxation of tensions*' [détente] can help us along . . . Meditation and disarmament discover a strategic common interest" (CCR 132). Obviously, philosophical humor seeks the same goal, but for Sloterdijk, disarmament is more generally a means to appease and defuse the conflicts and bivalences that traverse the history of ideas or of moral systems – what he calls the "de-radicalization of alternatives" (GZ 112).

This soothing effect is particularly sought after in the formulation of the notion of anthropotechnics (see chapter 2), which revisits the opposition between nature and culture to be able to overcome it. The reconciliation of alternatives stems from the idea that opposites are usually like spouses in a long-lasting marriage, that is, partners in conflict. The proposed disarmament lacks neither scope nor ambition and is not only interested in light or inoffensive cases. Indeed, this soothing effect even succeeds in effectively intruding upon the middle of a field as sensitive and explosive as battlefronts between and among the three monotheistic religions. In *God's Zeal: The Battle of the Three Monotheisms*, the only work he devoted to major religions, Sloterdijk looks into the possibilities of a happy coexistence among these cultural universes. In a rigorously skillful manner (see GZ 40–9), Sloterdijk dissects the 18 sub-conflicts entailed by the rivalries between and among Judaism, Christianity, and Islam, to which must be added three identity fronts (Jews, Christians, and Muslims) and their respective inherent opposi-tions to paganism and atheism. Against all expectations, the reader notes that these multiple confrontations are carriers of alliances more than of genuine rivalries, since the conflicts, claims Sloterdijk, often take the form of "two-against-one coalitions" (GZ 47). On the 18 bat-tlefronts, there is in fact a majority of allied forces, and in changing the makeup of these alliances, all of the actors involved – despite them-selves, perhaps – find themselves more often in a state of collaboration than of aggression. Although religious checks and balances constitute a base that is too uncertain for lasting peace, it is a first endogenous limit to the supremacism of each of the classical monotheisms that, paradoxically enough, "did not make the most of their polemogenic potential" (GZ 48).

This disarmament by default must also bear in mind all the non-combatant observers who do not participate in religious warfare or in the bivalent oppositions upholding it. Alongside the most reflexive fringe of each major religion, it is they who can found "schools of polyvalent thought" (GZ 118) within which humor – we come back to it again – will be the alpha discipline: "Humour can almost be consid-ered the school for polyvalence . . . This third view comes neither purely from below – from anxiety – nor purely from above – from indifference – but rather combines the upper and lower views in such a way that it has a liberating effect on the observer" (GZ 120).

Disarming bivalences is not merely a superficial stylistic or humor-istic undertaking. It lies at the very heart of the spirit infusing all of Sloterdijk's work. In this respect, the spherology project is the most ambitious undertaking that political thought has ever produced with a view to overcoming the opposition between the school of liberal individualism (contract theory) and the spiteful conservative school of holistic Romanticism (organicism). The poetics of spherology rearticu-lates the sense of belonging initially formulated by Romanticism, without sacrificing smaller units (couples, houses, tribes, and networks) in constituting contemporary social wholes.

Privileging patterns of belonging over those of the flow of neoliberal delocalization, Sloterdijk returns to his ever-present skepticism with regard to large-scale holistic enterprises, because of the risk that they claim the right to liquidate small and medium spherical agglomera-tions. In this regard, he warns that the too-weak reply given by the latest globalization to the question "What is it to inhabit?" will lead to a rearticulation of habitat thinking and a necessary rekindling of interest in the Small.

For the moment, the preliminary task consists in producing contemporary habitat thought that uses neither the language of abstract universalism (total de-spatialization) nor that of spiteful organicism (vegetal rootedness), to set the stage for a spatial paradigm that reveals the features and operative patterns of the contemporary organization of anthropogenic spaces. While the stakes of the old debate between contractual individualism and organic biologism were the monopoly of the plans for building the modern habitat at the start of the nineteenth century, Sloterdijk argues that we must now open up the terms of this debate, not to find a compromise but to show that both avenues use models based on a fiction that spherology seeks to refute. What is this fiction? Sloterdijk argues that it is the complete de-spatialization by these "inaugural" scenes that gave the initial impetus to these political fictions, thereby depriving them of any grasp of the real:

> In both contract theory and holism, we are faced with hyperboles indicative of the absence of declared constructivist considerations as such; although they are impressive, they abjure day-to-day reality, replacing it with elaborate versions of an abstract metaphor . . . Both contractualism and organicism are mistaken with regard to their object since they propose to enunciate the true reason for the being-together of humans with other humans without being able to produce a sensible word on the space within which this synthesis is achieved – and even less about the space opened up by this synthesis. Both are sightless in their spatial eye or again, more generally, in their situational or contextual eye. (SIII 287–8)

Here, Sloterdijk offers a disarmament of these two "enemy" trends – de-spatialization partners – while at the same time seeking, no doubt, to ward off any hasty lumping together of spherology and conservatism. The debate between the Enlightenment and Romanticism is revisited here to show that the two opponents share common defects: "While the fantasy of the contract brings falsified and colourless individuals together in an imaginary network, the organic fantasy grotesquely places people in a falsified and simplified 'whole'" (SIII 291). Sloterdijk goes to even greater lengths to distance himself from political, authoritarian Romanticism so as to remove all connections between his therapeutic approach and its caricatured and totalizing forgeries:

> In its way, organicist ideology destroys the meaning of the original specific spatialities of coexistence. It compresses neighbouring houses, microspheres, couples, teams and associations, populations and assemblies, the personnel in enterprises and classes into a hyper-body, as if the

coexistence of human bodies produced a higher-order vital composite.
(SIII 292)

In the self-designation of its project, spherology seeks, therefore, to go
beyond this ancient dualism, which, in fact, has never enabled us to
grasp the indomitable question of human space. Disarming the sterile
confrontation between liberalism and communitarianism makes it possible to reformulate the spatial question by asking: "Where are we
when we inhabit the global?" Such is the unimagined dimension of
globalization, the relevance of which Sloterdijk wants to bring to our
attention: "Belonging, *Zugehörigkeit, appartenance* – words like these
have good chances of becoming the losers' catchwords of the twenty-
first century. Needless to say, it is not least this that makes them some
of the most interesting terms of the future" (WIC 208).

Ecstatic Proximity

Projection into the Small

Spherological logic, which led us in chapter 3 to understand the absorp-
tion of the Small by the Big, leads us here to insist on the virtues of
strong belonging, that is, on the spherological project's most intimate
aspects and its therapeutic resonance in favor of ecstatic proximity and
projection into the Small.

It has been noted on a few occasions that despite all the attention
Sloterdijk pays to questions too big for him, the scale of the Big usually
gives way to the irreducible reality of the Small. The macroscopic is no
more than a pathway to the microscopic. Major planetary issues must
be re-rooted and re-territorialized so that we can re-learn how to think
at a much smaller scale about the bond and the site that forge and
engender humanness. Despite its initial grandiloquence, Sloterdijk's
grand narrative discourse always comes back to praising the irreducible human incubator, the blind spot of all large-scale politics. Henk
Oosterling argues that this necessary downsizing brings enormity
down to realistic proportions and makes it possible to combine micro-
political emancipation and the aesthetics of the monstrous, the two
faces of Sloterdijk's political thought that combine with one another in
the same undertaking: "Hyperpolitical megalopsychia becomes micro-
political inter-esse. In having rescaled and miniaturized megalopsychia
to these 'mediological' proportions, Sloterdijk's politico-aesthetic strategy is better understood as the micropolitics of public space, i.e. art as
public space."[16] For our part, this micro-political art is the very core of
Sloterdijk's therapeutic prescriptions, which, even though they might
be difficult to reconcile with the more vertical and hawkish aspects of
his more recent work, underlie a coherent, soothing vision of an

alter-modernity, the contours of which had already been expressed prior to 1800.

Magical intersubjectivity

Sloterdijk's interest in the last quarter of the eighteenth century stems from the fact that this period was characterized by a diversity of de-subjectivizing and therapeutic experiences that still resisted bourgeois individualism and continued to explore the "magical" patterns of intersubjectivity:

> Long before the axioms of individualistic abstraction established themselves, the psychologist-philosophers of the early Modern Age had made it clear that the interpersonal space was overcrowded with symbiotic, erotic and mimetic-competitive energies that fundamentally deny the illusion of subject autonomy. (B 207)

For Sloterdijk, the field of these forgotten experiments has once again become fertile for an archaeology of forms of human relationship and belonging, the occlusion of which has been helped along by the modernist narrative. In this vein, *Bubbles* strives to provide a history of small human entities – intimate loves and other forms of holistic communes – that are the primitive incubators and psycho-reactors of strong relationships: "love stories are stories of form, and . . . every act of solidarity is an act of sphere formation, that is to say the creation of an interior" (B 12). This site is that of the microspheres, a space in which thermodynamic relations can take form. The apolitical tone of this first spherological study is well in line with Sloterdijk's general preference for small, incandescent enclosures that give birth to more significant human relationships. In the absence of *Große Politik* (Big Politics), Sloterdijk focus here on small entities so as to be able to continue to reflect upon the first reasons for what can still bond human beings:

> Thus an inquiry into our location is more productive than ever, as it examines the place that humans create in order to have somewhere they can appear as those who they are . . . The sphere is the interior, disclosed, shared realm inhabited by humans – in so far as they succeed in becoming humans. Because living always means building spheres, both on a small and a large scale, humans are the beings that establish globes and look out into horizons. Living in spheres means creating the dimension in which humans can be contained. Spheres are immune-systematically effective space creations for ecstatic beings that are operated upon by the outside. (B 28)

Whoever examines the sphere identifies the site of production of bonds. This therapeutic, which helps with a micro-political emancipation, cannot avoid a critique of the individualism that perpetually inhibits our understanding of relations of proximity. For this reason, Sloterdijk does not hesitate to diagnose individualism as a *modern illness* stemming from a denial of the Other and Being-with. To overcome this illness, it strikes Sloterdijk as necessary to consider the antithesis of individualism – the sphere of meeting – as a therapeutic intrusion of the Other into the Self or as a dissolution of the Self into the Other.

The malaise: the modern as aggression

Sloterdijk's undertaking consists in understanding and drawing out the ecstatic bonds linking "individuals" by way of a space, a habitat, or a site. The basic intuition here stems from the idea that *only human beings are possessed or possessing beings*, because "stones lying beside one another are unfamiliar with reciprocal ecstatic openness" (SIII 14–15).

The ensuing analytic task requires not only the reactivation of the Romantics' familiar complaint about the Enlightenment's abstract universalism, but also and above all the rediscovery of the constitutive envelopes of human existence – bonds, neighborhoods, and houses – by reconsidering all of modernity's premises with regard to the fictive genesis of delocalized individuals. In this light, Sloterdijk wonders what we could expect to find before this philosophy of bonds, neighborhoods, and houses other than a modern malaise that systematically participates in denying these three patterns of belonging. He argues that this denial is precisely a denial of the unity of form and matter, of bond and site, that lies at the heart of modern discourse and militant humanisms (see chapter 2). As such, microspherology revisits the pernicious history of this rupture of form and content such as it was brought about by moderns in the genesis of the fiction of individualism.

The major features of modern narratives of the birth of the state depict all human beings as individuals locked in a battle for survival and to varying degrees in a state of war. In this sombre portrait, we immediately note that the denial of bonds, neighborhoods, and houses lies at the heart of modernity. These narratives present a largely fictional account of a "pure" individual that "gave birth to itself," is "solitary" and without "Being-with." Thenceforward, this individuality, bereft of an envelope and stripped of all spirit (or what the Greeks referred to as *daimon*), was held aloft as a major issue for modern political thought because the nakedness of its elementary particles meant that they must be immunized against the world. Sloterdijk argues that it is precisely at this point in the story that the modern myth of individuality begins to turn sour. It engenders regrettable consequences, such as that all the inaugural scenes of the modern mentality must ultimately prescribe a sort of immunization that can be produced only by suspicion and aggression.

Be it Descartes's immunity via radical doubt, Rousseau's misanthropic immunity of self-sufficient, natural human beings, or Hobbes's complete absence of immunity found in human beings caught up in a war of all against all, Sloterdijk finds that these foundational narratives share the same discourse, in which individuals are beings that are allergic to others and the environment and that must battle them to ensure their own survival (by virtue of their inalienable right to self-preservation). In the narrative's ensuing logic, individuals transfer, via a contractualist mechanism, this presumed survival obligation to the state itself, with the result that suspicion and aggression assume an unprecedentedly gigantic scale of destructiveness. In the twentieth century, these large immune systems that we commonly refer to as states pushed this self-preservation imperative (along with its tendency to suspicion, hostility, and aggression) to assume pathologically radical forms of modern mentality by means of state cynicism: generalized espionage (cheat so as not to be cheated) and the proliferation of nuclear bombs (destroy before being destroyed).

Soothing dyads

By linking these disastrous consequences to the fallacious principles of modern individualism, Sloterdijk seeks to counter this narrative. He presents his own anti-individualist, anthropogenic narrative, which includes not already-individualized beings but basically dyadic beings that have a much more plausible existence than any imagined individuality. Whereas modern narratives wonder *what* the attributes of a singular individual are, spherology asks *where* human beings are, and in doing so draws out the fact that human beings are creators of spaces and cannot live anywhere else than in their own animated spaces.

In the introduction to *Schäume* (*Foams*), Sloterdijk argues that being in a sphere signifies that "the couple is a dimension that is more real than the individual – which also signifies that the immunity of Us incarnates a deeper phenomenon than the immunity of I" (SIII 13).[17] In Sloterdijk's view, all human phenomena are minimally dyadic because the I is always duplicated – by an image in a mirror, by a relationship with God, by a dialogue with oneself, and, in the case of unmarried singles, by the fusion they maintain with their apartment and their medial equipment.[18] In this light, even states at war are partners in conflict. On the one hand, the dyadic structure acts as a principle of phenomenological observation that underlies the entire spherological project. On the other hand, it refutes the fiction of the self-sufficient individual by wanting to develop another immunological narrative that might be able once again to induce therapeutic resonances.

At the micro-analytic level, the spherology of intimacy debunks the myth of the modern individual through a counter-therapy of strong bonds. To this end, it takes a forgotten vocabulary of interactions and attractions from magician-thinkers such as Giordano Bruno:

> The bond thus consists in a certain correspondence not only between the members amongst themselves, but also in a certain corresponding dis-position of the captor and the captive . . . The bond does not capture the soul unless it can tie and bind; it does not bind it unless it reaches it; and it does not reach it unless it can be captured by something. In general the bond reaches the soul through knowledge, ties it through the affect, attracts it through pleasure.[19] (B 219)

Bubbles reveals a series of conceptions of the world that have been repressed and sublimated by de-spatialized modern discourse. Never-theless, this discourse continues to haunt the aggressive immunology of moderns by presenting another version of history:

> The central law of intersubjectivity as experienced in premodern atti-tudes is the enchantment of humans through humans . . . Among humans, fascination is the rule and disenchantment the exception . . . Where phi-losophy of the early Modern Age mentions such effects of resonance and infection, it spontaneously draws on the vocabulary of *magological* tradi-tions. (B 207–8)

Alongside Bruno, thinkers such as Marsile Ficin and, later, Franz Anton Mesmer all contributed to this psychology of the depths, the "magical" rules of which systematically belied the autonomy of the rational subject. Mesmer's Romantic medicine even left his name to a fashion-able therapy that consciously sought to de-individualize sick subjects by inducing hypnotic crises. Mesmer's theory of animal magnetism, the principles of which were compiled by Karl Wolfart, fascinated a range of people as surprising and varied as Lafayette, Washington, Humboldt, Hegel, and Schopenhauer.

Magnetism

Mesmer's magnetopathic treatment is not a psychology of the indi-vidual. Rather, it seeks to undermine the foundations of the counter-natural individual that strives to maintain itself to the point of weakening the patient's body. Magnetic therapy attempts to break down the barriers between individuals in order to destroy the obstacles to the circulation of magnetic fluid in the sick:

> There is a fixed law of nature that a reciprocal influence on all bodies exists, and this consequently affects all their constituent parts and

properties. This reciprocal influence and the relationships between all coexistent bodies constitute what one calls magnetism . . . There is only one sickness and only one cure; health consists in the complete harmony of all our organs and their functions. Sickness is merely deviation from this harmony. The cure therefore consists in restoring the harmony that has been disturbed. No sickness can be cured without crisis; the crisis is the striving of nature to disperse the obstacles inhibiting the circulation by an increase in movement, tone and tension.[20] (B 226–8)

Sloterdijk argues that magnetism's curative art represented the avant-garde in the Dionysian subversion of aggressive and suspicious individualism. As he notes, however, while the subject was effectively disarmed in this manner, he or she did not passively fall under the "tutelage" of the therapist: "As far as the magnetopathic approach is concerned, the precondition for this was indeed that the patients, as the magnetizing doctor's unconscious assistants, would become their own co-therapists" (B 244). Sloterdijk's sympathy for this infatuation with magnetism up until the early nineteenth century led him to add that, far from leading to a loss of autonomy, this therapeutic movement explored areas in which the pattern of individuality could be compatible with health: "For a valuable precarious moment, philosophical-medical thought attained a complete balance of autonomy and devotion" (B 242).

Primal companion

Sloterdijk also shows that the aggressiveness of modern individualism has a medical counterpart in gynecological terms,. To illustrate the clinical creation of the sovereign Self in the age of holistic discourses and exploratory de-subjectivization in another way, he examines the symptomatic destiny of the placenta, which becomes the organic metaphor of the modern denial of bonds, neighborhoods, and houses: "Bourgeois-individualist positivism established – against weak resistance from exponents of soul-partnership Romanticism – the radical, imaginary solitary confinement of individuals in the womb, the cot and their own skin throughout society" (B 384).

This state of affairs reveals another facet of memories repressed in the birth of the modern *atopos* individual. What the Germans used to call *der Urbegleiter* (the primal companion) is now forgotten. However, up until the mid-eighteenth century, the placenta was generally viewed as the child's double, its own *daimon* in a shared birth. Consequently, it was treated with a high degree of ritual (buried under the house, in the garden, under a fruit tree, etc.):

All births are twin births; no one comes into the world unaccompanied or unattached. Every arrival who ascends to the light is followed by a

Eurydice – anonymous, mute and not made to be beheld. What will remain, namely the individual that cannot be separated again, is already the product of a separating cut that divides the previously inseparable parties into the child and the remainder. (B 413–14)

However, by the end of the eighteenth century, bourgeois medicine did away with these rituals. In this new era, the placenta was excommunicated and made into an object of disgust. The child's double no longer existed and had become, rather, organic waste: "In terms of its psychodynamic source, the individualism of the Modern Age is a placental nihilism" (B 387).

This symptom is highly significant for the spherology of bubbles. Firstly, it concretely shows the medical creation of a first without a second, of a pure, born-alone individual without "Being-with." Secondly, it helps us to understand what was mobilized by political theory to take charge of the intra-uterine bubble's immunological functions in order to transfer them to the authority of the state. In sum, this transfer of the incubating features of a given habitat to another – such is the pattern of spherical constructions – can succeed if and only if small entities come to be viewed, for dubious good reasons and in questionable good faith, as "obsolete."

However, notes Sloterdijk, microspheres never completely disappear from the register of bonds, neighborhoods, and houses because the spherology of the Small multiplies observations and monitors their permanence and their close link with the sustainability of the intimate. The site of this micro-belonging – uterine, loving, ecstatic, vocal, religious, and musical – is a spatial refutation of the de-spatialized constitutions of modernity. This Romantic counter-narrative can thus be viewed, in turn, as rationalism's placenta. Even though Romanticism and the Enlightenment share a modern birth, the latter excommunicated the former and for too long saw itself as the debate's only winner and the only heir to the modern project. As counter-heir and by way of his poeticization of lived space, Sloterdijk works to produce a conception of the world that takes the best from Romanticism in order to provide it with a renewed presence. In an uncertain global age, the conviction that emancipated life must arise out of small entities recalls, to be sure, the Schlegelian ideal that, when faced with the deployment of Napoleonic *Große Politik*, believed that a global alliance of creators represented a kind of association in line with the requirements of the time: "Where the artists form a family, there are the original assemblies of humanity."[21]

Solar Language

One of Sloterdijk's most enjoyable works is *Nietzsche Apostle*, a homage he delivered as a speech at Weimar for the centenary of Nietzsche's death. This small book is a concentrate of therapeutic proposals for all those whose profession it is to produce discourse. Although this commemorative occasion was another opportunity for him to reaffirm his faithfulness to his inimitable master, the book proposes a liberating thesis with regard to the function of language: despite the denial and false humility of the sacerdotal-intellectual caste, language has never served any other purpose than self-praise.

It is in this sense that Nietzsche is described as "a catastrophe in the history of language" (NA 8), because he offers as a gift the "total sponsoring" (NA 47) of one who, rid of this mechanism of denial, radiates in the full joviality of eulogy and self-praising language:

> When used in accordance with its constitutive function of primary narcissism, language says one and the same thing over and again: that nothing better could have happened to the speaker than, precisely, to have been who he is, to have been who he is at this place and in this language, and to bear witness to the merit of his being in his own skin. (NA 9)

One must be able to love oneself a great deal to topple centuries of ressentiment and struggle against pride in order to allow oneself to sing one's own praises and to construct oneself as an object of admiration. Such was Nietzsche's exemplary exploit.

Nietzsche's so-called megalomania, which reaches a summit in the pages of *Ecce homo*, stems not from mental illness but from phenomenal ambition: to blow up the bank of language. In this regard, Nietzsche had a few precursors in speech-writing who came close to rising to the task. Sloterdijk argues that the so-called Jefferson Bible anticipated in a rough, indirect way Nietzsche's future observation with regard to the fact that the finest discursive and creative forces are still walled up and turned away from their full potential, even at the height of the modern age. An enlightened man and a great rationalist, Thomas Jefferson gave himself the quasi-role of writer of the Gospels by manufacturing a private copy of them in which all enchanted or incongruous passages were removed: "This is the meaning of neo-humanism: to be able to eliminate in the old Gospel that which has become incompatible with one's own glorification as a humanist and citizen" (NA 21). However, this eulogy, by way of removal or subtraction, only half-guesses the ultimate power of language in the creation of political and moral orders. It is an indirect glorification that works only by the misuse of consecrated sources. Be it a bowdlerized version of the Bible or of literary or philosophical canons, the source's authority requires an act of humility by one who would quote it: "'One who is humble will be elevated', or *servir et disparaître*" (NA 52).

The major catastrophe orchestrated by Nietzsche consisted in completing what the moderns had only half finished, namely transforming indirect eulogy into direct eulogy and rewriting the Gospels in a tone in which humility is absent. Such is the sense of the *Fifth Gospel*, otherwise known as *Thus Spoke Zarathustra*: "it is a beautiful story: I have challenged all the religions and made a new 'holy book'! And, said in all seriousness, it is as serious as any other, even though it incorporates laughter into religion"[22] (NA 30). There is no parody in this laughter. Sloterdijk considers quite seriously Nietzsche's seriousness in this undertaking: "The author of *Zarathustra* wanted to lay here the eulogistic force of language from the ground up, and to free it from the inhibitions with which resentment, itself coded by metaphysics, had stamped it" (NA 33). The portended catastrophe was in fact the most generous of gifts and became the antidote to "the abasement of the happy and powerful, and of self-praising attitudes" (NA 34).

Nietzsche's conception of eulogistic language breaks not only with metaphysics, but also with all stances that maintain a suspicious or miserly relationship to language. In contrast to Freud's apprehensive vision, the essence of language is not to betray the genuine desires of a patient whose utterances are demeaned in clinical practice.[23] In contrast to the persistence of humility in the world of scholars and their strategic investments in the publications stock exchange, Nietzsche's total expenditure is a game changer. It is no longer a matter of an economy of investors, but one of donors and sponsors. Nietzsche, aka Sloterdijk, makes the sun shine on ethical models:

> The sun alone is heroic right to the moment of setting and remains generous until it goes down . . . Only suns can be so profligate that they can be placed under the guardianship of rational heirs, when the economic ideas of the latter manage to prevail. Only the sun has a giving virtue as first nature; only suns care nothing for the symmetry between giving and taking; only suns shine sovereignty over proponents and opponents; and only suns read no critiques. (NA 78)

Nietzsche's ethical exigencies go beyond the critique of metaphysics and the old Gospels of humility. He helps Sloterdijk to decode what is really at work in the writing of the Gospels and in the founding of religions. When Sloterdijk provides a better idea of what he had explored in *You Must Change Your Life* and *God's Zeal*, he argues that all religions adopt the "Sinai scheme" underlying Judaism; they found a sacred discourse and a national or civilizational belonging simultaneously: "Through the Sinai scheme, a people can surpass itself with the help of a programmatic institution that demands total belonging and a strict oath of allegiance to an ethical and cultural project."[24] The three monotheisms created such ethical and cultural entities: the Israel of Judaism; the ecclesia or congregation of Christianity; and the *ummah wāhidah* (one community or commonwealth of believers) of Islam. For

Nietzsche, the creation of an ethical people is the ultimate "speech act," the strong expression of the will to create and give itself a set of values.

Theology provides only the slightest of glimpses of this power. It is for this reason that Sloterdijk prefers to compare these founding moments to theatrical science and the invention of new mental exercises and rituals. Viewed from the perspective of their autoplasticity, religions have much to do with "theopoetry." Indeed, they are among "the most important manifestations of the earth's most poetic habitats."[25] To study this kind of poetry up close, one must draw on a few other forerunners, such as William James. In contrast to Freud's pettiness with regard to the infantile nature of religious sentiment, they developed a "non-dogmatic interest in religion."[26] For Sloterdijk, the fact of religion is also related to spherology's immunological function. It must be constantly emulated and rearticulated within the paths taken by humanity, which has to incubate itself without salvation, if not beyond salvation.

Getting back to Nietzsche's Gospel, the heart of the matter consists of an invitation to go beyond shortfalls, calculations, and assets and liabilities in the ultimate exercise of creating both oneself and the world. It is this idea of true altruistic giving that Sloterdijk had in mind when he very maladroitly presented it as an abstract solution to a complex and concrete fiscal and income tax problem (see chapter 4). In an artistic, psychological, and moral frame, Nietzsche's solar ethic has a much more powerful sense. Transplanted into New World thought, it becomes Emerson's self-reliance. Trusting one's own genius leads to the multiplication of fortifying and healthy radiating hubs for all adherents to this ethic of generosity. The sun can be warmed only by other suns, who collectively expend their creative fire to the point of total expenditure without setting aside any savings:

> I am penetrated therefore I am; I radiate in you, therefore you are. By sexualizing the sun, [Nietzsche] reverses the direction of imitation and compels the sun to become the imitator of people, provided that the individual is an author – that is, one who is penetrated by language, by music, a voice, which seeks ears and creates them. (NA 80)

Conclusion

This book has sought to present an exhaustive portrait of Sloterdijk's thought. To this end, I have attempted to reveal the many and varied roles he has assumed throughout the body of his work: psychologist, anthropologist, spherologist, lightning rod for scandals, and formulator of therapeutic prescriptions. The book's five chapters cover the various aspects of these roles and anti-roles, all the while revealing on each occasion that Sloterdijk's persona is ineluctably linked to his written work. As Heine noted so well in his irreverent and caustic portrait of the major figures of German idealism, a thinker's philosophical temperament is not a philosophical footnote or an improper view of a noble activity. Rather, it goes directly to the heart of his or her work. In incorporating Heine's perspective into his own portraits of illustrious philosophers, Sloterdijk maintains that "submissive souls opt for a naturalistic system that justifies their servility, while individuals with a proud disposition reach for a system of freedom."[1] This book makes the acquaintance of an author who is lacking neither in pride nor in ambition and is among the most provocative and daring philosophers alive today. By way of conclusion, a few nuances are added to this portrait and Sloterdijk's work is situated within the framework of serene observation and serendipity.

"[A] man never climbs higher than when he does not know where is going" (MCL 176). As legend has it, the three princes of Serendip made their discoveries only by accident, though they had to be sagacious enough to weave apparently disparate facts into to a coherent whole. Knowledge is an adventure, and the school of serendipity always requires "exploits of observation and inference" on the part of travelers.[2] In his capacity as a physician of culture, coach, or oracle, Sloterdijk strives to be an "observer who watches others' actions intelligently" (AP 82), that is, a practitioner of eccentric intelligence. Doing so is no easy task, especially for someone who is so committed to being in the public eye and the object of the sometimes violent judgments of his fellow citizens. To attain serenity by way of serendipity, shouldn't our therapist also ultimately comply with some elements of therapy?

As an intellectual project, serendipity not only looks outward, but also takes into account the researcher's participation in his or her research object. We can see a turn to serendipity in the social sciences because of the reflexive taking into consideration of these kinds of affective, intuitive, self-experimental, and certainly "deviant" (relative to classical rationalism) linkages.[3] In this respect, Sloterdijk is once again a trailblazer who is never more apposite and incisive than when he speaks about what he has observed as an observer who is immersed in, and willingly intoxicated by, what he is studying. However, this kind of immersive participation is only one aspect of the act of observing as defined by the recent Sloterdijk. When he defines observation as an exercise in *The Art of Philosophy*, Sloterdijk reintroduces a needed distance in the postphenomenological project. In this regard, he appears to want to devote himself to Husserl and his concept of *epoché* – stepping back. Such is the therapist's therapy.

Observation is firstly an act of observance. It presupposes a "disinterested person" (AP 61) who is light years away from existential involvement. Unable to resist his polemical libido, Sloterdijk adds that neutral reason has little chance of seeing the light of day because it must be able to resist assassination attempts on a hostile way. Among the assassins are Marx, Bourdieu, Butler, and Lukács, who require thinkers "to take up positions on the front line of the longest struggle" (AP 88). On the darker side of things, Nietzsche and Heidegger – whom Sloterdijk rarely critiques – display excessive regionalism in their critique of universalism. None of these critiques – to which must be added the sociology of knowledge and derivatives of military science – can be completely ignored. Nor can any one of them be exclusively followed to ensure a principle of free observation.

A principle of this kind resides instead in *epoché*, also defined as *Scheintod* (apparent death), a state of torpor or of clairvoyant sleep that, in contrast to the agitation of militancy, allows itself a short stay in a neutral country. This state is not permanent. It is *apparent* death and does not give access to Plato's fantasized world of intelligible and eternal forms. Neither a zombie nor a zealot, the thinker is, rather, in a state of suspended animation. This presence/absence is a distinct practice in the vast library of human exercises, and can only be an acrobatic exaggeration, an attempt to reach a higher region in the repository of language. It asks for an eccentric discipline and someone with a touch of melancholy who no longer believes in angels:

Even in today's world, regardless of many problematic developments, philosophy and science are practiced as noble exercises of conscious life, although the naive ideology of angels has played out its role. The true players of life in the theoretical professions demonstrate by daily example that there must be a third option between death and the common lot. (AP 94)

The attentive reader will no doubt see the irony in this invitation to temper passions in the course of scholarly activities, especially when it comes from an *enfant terrible* of contemporary German philosophy. The provocateur seeks peace and withdraws himself like a subdued Rousseau examining the flowers in his garden in moments of solitary reverie. This post-controversy rest also recalls the one taken by another figure whose laughter was a source of considerable inspiration for the young Sloterdijk. After the publication of *Eichmann in Jerusalem,* Hannah Arendt too came to appreciate the spectator's point of view with regard to human affairs and devoted herself anew to philosophy, her first profession. Thus our philosopher in retreat remains true to the Epicurean stance, which is still his most constant ideal, notwithstanding his other passing prescriptions – or at least one hopes these prescriptions are indeed passing – in favor of thymotic heroism and agonistic polemics.

In a world devoured by cynicism and powerlessness, the garden is a miniature city composed of elective affinities that seek the collective cultivation of the discipline of a healthy mind in a healthy body. To this end, the cosmology of Epicurus postulates that human beings can reflect the freedom of each of the atoms that make up the universe. Humans are able to imitate *clinamen*, the spontaneous and unpredictable freedom of an atomic swerve, and change lives in this life. Sloterdijk's seductiveness stems not only from his stylistic prowess, but also and ultimately from the fact that he lives in accordance with what he thinks. Those who refuse to write under surveillance make a gift of their *autarkeia* – the self-reliance of a healthy love of the self – to a young public that has not yet resigned itself to complying with the norms of the scholarly industry.

With a view to tempering the sympathy for and admiration of Sloterdijk's jovial megalomania, this book has also provided a critical reading of his tendency to always oppose exceptional beings to the masses. This Nietzschean, vertical characteristic inevitably puts him on a collision course with the foundations of democracy. Although an author's temperament does indeed shed light on the foundations of his or her thought, and while it is impossible for an aging writer to subsume or overcome herself or himself, it is worth bearing in mind the choicest gems of this philosophical performance, not to mention the laughter it has inspired and the new worlds that it has opened up.

Notes

Introduction

1 In addition to several articles, Tuinen published *Peter Sloterdijk: Ein Profil* (Paderborn: Fink, 2007) as well as a special issue on Peter Sloterdijk for *Cultural Politics* 3 (3) 2007. For his part, Heinrichs published *Peter Sloterdijk: Die Kunst des Philosophierens* (Munich: Hanser, 2011) and, with Sloterdijk, a collection of interviews translated as *Neither Sun nor Death*, transl. S. Corcoran (Los Angeles: Semiotext(e), 2011).

2 Sloterdijk, "Postface à l'édition française de *Règles pour le parc humain*" [Afterword to "Rules for the Human Zoo"] (Paris: Mille et une nuits, 1999), 57.

3 To underline this unabashed francophilia, he published all his writings on this theme in a single collection titled *Mein Frankreich* [*My France*] (Berlin: Suhrkamp, 2013).

4 Tuinen, *Peter Sloterdijk*, 139.

5 Sloterdijk and Alain Finkielkraut, *Les battements du monde* (Paris: Pauvert, 2003).

6 Régis Debray invited Sloterdijk to inaugurate the Emmanuel-Levinas Chair at the University of Strasbourg in 2005. His keynote address was published as "What Happened in the Twentieth Century? En Route to a Critique of Extremist Reason," *Cultural Politics* 3 (3) 2007: 327–56.

7 Appointed associate director of the Institut d'études politiques de Paris in 2007, Latour is a philosopher of science and an anthropologist of culture. With regard to his intellectual intimacy with his German friend, he candidly admits that "I was born a Sloterdijkian" (Bruno Latour, "Spheres and Networks: Two Ways to Reinterpret Globalization," *Harvard Design Magazine* 30 2009: 138–44 at 139).

8 Sloterdijk, *Derrida, An Egyptian*, transl. W. Hoban (Cambridge: Polity, 2009).

9 See Boris Groys and Peter Weibel (eds.), *Medium Religion: Faith. Religion. Art* (Cologne: König, 2011); Bruno Latour and Peter Weibel (eds.), *Making Things Public: Atmospheres of Democracy* (Cambridge MA: MIT Press, 2005);

Bruno Latour, Peter Weibel, and Charlotte Bigg (eds.), *Iconoclash: Beyond the Image Wars in Science, Religion, and Art* (Cambridge MA: MIT Press, 2002).

10 Taken from www.petersloterdijk.net (December 23, 2012).

11 Albert William Levi, *Philosophy as Social Expression* (Chicago: University of Chicago Press, 1974).

12 Sloterdijk, *Die Verachtung der Massen: Versuch über Kulturkämpfe in der modernen Gesellschaft* (Frankfurt am Main: Suhrkamp, 2000), 62–3.

Chapter 1   Psychopolitics

1 Psychopolitics is also important in the case of post-war stress (TPWP) and can be linked to the "climatological" analysis of the luxury society (WIC, SIII).

2 The Weimar Republic (1918–33) is the name given to Germany's unstable democratic regime following World War I and dissolved by the Nazis. Article 1 of its constitution, which was written at Weimar and dated August 11, 1919, stipulated that "the German Reich is a Republic" (*Das Deutsche Reich ist eine Republik*).

3 The year in which Puységur's memoirs on magnetic treatments were published. See Marquis de Puységur, *Mémoires pour servir à l'histoire et à l'établissement du magnétisme animal* (Paris: L'Harmattan, 2008).

4 The intensity and mimicry that make up Sloterdijk's relationship with Nietzsche (see Dalie Giroux, "Nietzsche et Sloterdijk, corps en resonance," *Horizons philosophiques* 17 [2] 2007: 101–22) should not be attributed to a far-fetched metempsychosis. However, it should be noted that Sloterdijk is the most Nietzschean philosopher of our times, and our times are the most Nietzschean in the history of philosophy. Since the philologist-evangelist's conquest of professorial philosophy in the latter half of the twentieth century, there has been a proliferation of the nephews of Zarathustra (Louis Pinto, *Les neveux de Zarathoustra* [Paris: Seuil, 1995]), and in this lot of copier-imitators, Sloterdijk's Germanness, literacy, and bitingly jovial irony stand out and place him in a position to pick up the baton of the philosopher-artist in the present day.

5 "Weimar et la Californie: note sur la crise de la philosophie de l'histoire et sur la prolifération des doctrines holistiques," *Critique* 464–5 1986: 114–27.

6 "Weimar et la Californie," 118.

7 "Weimar et la Californie," 118.

8 "Weimar et la Californie," 125. Sloterdijk refers here to material analyzed in his doctoral thesis.

9 "Weimar et la Californie," 127.

10 Friedrich Nietzsche, "On the Uses and Disadvantages of History for Life," in Nietzsche, *Untimely Meditations* (Cambridge: Cambridge University Press, 1997), 95. I wish to thank my colleague Robert Hébert for this reference to this work, which clarifies most of Sloterdijk's presuppositions in his conception of history.

11 Nietzsche, "On the Uses and Disadvantages of History for Life," 120.

12 Nietzsche, "On the Uses and Disadvantages of History for Life," 89–90.

13 Nietzsche, "On the Uses and Disadvantages of History for Life," 83.

14 For Kant, the autonomy of the subject must overcome the "self-incurred minority": "*Minority* is *the* inability to make use of one's own understanding without direction from another. This minority is *self-incurred* when its cause lies not in lack of understanding but in lack of resolution and courage to use it without direction from another" (Immanuel Kant, "An Answer to the Question: What is Enlightenment?" in Kant, *Practical Philosophy* [Cambridge: Cambridge University Press, 1996], 17). Sloterdijk exploits this through analogies.

15 Rüdiger Safranski, "Peter Sloterdijk: Meister der fröhlich en Wissenschaft," *Die Welt*, June 26, 2007. In reference to *Critique of Cynical Reason*, Safranski also wrote: "As is well known, ten years earlier we had already ineptly and dogmatically attempted this removal from society. However, with this book and this author, the brilliant irony of the best of the romantic school made its grand entrance."

16 As Sloterdijk notes: "I began writing [*Critique of Cynical Reason*] shortly after seeing an interview with the Jewish philosopher and political scientist, Hannah Arendt . . . One must have heard with one's own ears how this woman averred that in studying the many thousands of pages of the transcript of the proceedings [of the Jerusalem trial of the mass murderer Adolf Eichmann], she repeatedly broke out into loud laughter about the peculiar stupidity that has exercised control over innumerable lives . . . then I also had to laugh, and with that, this book began to 'write itself'" (CCR 299).

17 See Ian Kershaw, *The Nazi Dictatorship: Problems and Perspectives of Interpretation* (London: Arnold Press, 2000).

18 This stance could be perceived as somewhat scandalous when, for example, Heidegger let slip the following:

> Agriculture is now a motorized food industry, the same thing in its essence as the production of corpses in the gas chambers and the extermination camps, the same thing as blockades and the reduction of countries to famine, the same thing as the manufacture of hydrogen bombs. (Heidegger quoted by Donald E. Pease, "Foreword," in William V. Spanos, *Heidegger and Criticism: Retrieving the Cultural Politics of Destruction* [Minneapolis: University of Minnesota Press, 1993], xiii)

However, when Sloterdijk works the same ground when discussing the overabundance characteristic of consumer society, he adopts Heidegger's position (without, however, alluding to it):

> The main emphasis of the current exploitation has moved to livestock, for which the industrialization of farming brought about the age of massive production and use. On this subject, statistics are more informative than sentimental arguments: according to the German government's 2003 Animal Welfare Report, almost 400 million chickens were slaughtered in 2002, along with 31 million turkeys and nearly 14 million ducks; of large mammals, 44.3 million pigs, 4.3 million cows and 2.1 million sheep and goats met their final use . . . The monstrous scale of the figures exceeds any affective judgment – nor do analogies to the martial holocausts of the National Socialists, the Bolshevists and the Maoists fully reflect the unfathomable routines in the production and use of animal carcasses. (WIC 230)

19 After the Nuremberg trials, the jurist Carl Schmitt (1888–1985) was barred from teaching. Although Sloterdijk never mentions his name in *Critique of Cynical Reason*, Schmitt corresponds perfectly to the symptoms of hegemonic cynicism. A Nazi sympathizer who refused his denazification, he became a major conservative political philosopher by advocating an absolutist concept of state sovereignty. In his view, the failure of Nazism in no way diminished the permanence of the problem of the need for indivisible authority in the modern state. See Carl Schmitt, *Political Theology: Four Chapters on the Concept of Sovereignty* (Chicago: University of Chicago Press, 2004).

20 Jean-Pierre Faye, *L'État total selon Carl Schmitt: ou comment la narration engendre des monstres* (Paris: Germina, 2013), 138.

21 Max Horkheimer, "Egoism and Freedom Movements: On the Anthropology of the Bourgeois Era," in Horkheimer, *Between Philosophy and Social Science* (Cambridge MA: MIT Press, 1993), 96. In addition, Horkheimer's flagship work, *Eclipse of Reason* (1944), resonates with Sloterdijk's, who parodies the title of his 1967 German translation, *Zur Kritik der instrumentellen Vernunft* [*Critique of Instrumental Reason*].

22 Jean-François Lyotard, *The Postmodern Condition: A Report on Knowledge* (Minneapolis: University of Minnesota Press, 1984).

23 Sloterdijk adopts this usage from Heinrich Niehues-Pröbsting, *Der Kynismus der Diogenes und der Begriff des Zynismus* (Munich: Wilhelm Fink, 1979).

24 Lucian of Samosata, the Mocker, is the prototype of insolence that changed sides. Confronted with Peregrinus' neokynical pressure, he proposed a "satire" to comfort established authorities when they were the objects of criticism: "Lucian's laughter remains a nuance too shrill to be serene; it reveals more hate than sovereignty. In there is the sarcasm of someone who feels himself put on the spot" (CCR 174).

25 For more details of Sloterdijk's portrayal of Diogenes, see CCR 101–7, 156–69.

26 However, Babette Babich feels that Sloterdijk's fixation on urinating in public is very much a masculine vision of kynical transgression. See Babette Babich, "Sloterdijk's Cynicism: Diogenes in the Marketplace," in S. Elden (ed.), *Sloterdijk Now* (Cambridge: Polity, 2012), 22.

27 The irony is as follows: while one author was emerging (Sloterdijk) and another was on the point of disappearing (Foucault), for the first and only time the latter mentioned the name of his young German colleague, on February 29, 1984, when he referred to: "a book, by someone called Sloterdijk, which someone pointed out to me recently, but which I have not read, appeared last year in Germany, published by Suhrkamp, and bears the solemn title *Kritik der zynischen Vernunft* (*Critique of Cynical Reason*). No critique of reason will be spared us, not of pure, or of dialectical, or of political reason, and so we have: 'critique of cynical reason.' It is a book in two volumes about which I know nothing. I have been given some, let's say, divergent views on the book's interest." Michel Foucault, *The Courage of Truth: The Government of Self and Others II. Lectures at the Collège de France 1983–1984* (New York: Palgrave Macmillan, 2011), 179.

28 "We will find a reliably unreliable traveling companion in Heinrich Heine, who displayed a knack, unsurpassed to the present day, for combining theory and satire, cognition and entertainment. Here, following in his

tracks, we want to try to reunite the capacities for truth in literature, satire and art with those of 'scholarly discourse'" (CCR 18).

29 Rüdiger Safranski, *Romantik: Eine deutsche Affäre* (Munich: Hanser, 2007), 253.

30 Heinrich Heine, *The Harz Journey and Selected Prose* (London: Penguin, 2006), 211.

31 Freud sees Heine as an author who had the courage to defy the inanities of morality, such as the one that stipulated that we must love our enemies:

> I have the most peaceable disposition. My wishes are: a modest cottage with a thatched roof, but a good bed, good food, milk and butter, flowers in front of the window, a few beautiful trees in front of the door; and if the good lord wants to make me completely happy, he will grant me the pleasure of seeing six or seven of my enemies hung from these trees. My heart will be moved, and before they die I will forgive them all the wrongs they did me in their lifetime. Yes, one must forgive one's enemies, but not before they are hanged. (Heine quoted by Sigmund Freud, *Civilization and Its Discontents* [London: Penguin, 2002], 52)

32 "People will one day say that Heine and I were by far the foremost artists of the German language – incalculably far beyond everything mere Germans have done with it." Friedrich Nietzsche, *Ecce homo* (Oxford: Oxford University Press, 2007), 25–6.

33 For the ethical implications of Nietzsche's writing according to Sloterdijk, see chapter 5.

34 Jean-Pierre Lefebvre, "Présentation," in Heinrich Heine, *Histoire de la religion et de la philosophie en Allemagne* (Paris: Imprimerie nationale, 1993), 9.

35 Theodor Adorno and Max Horkheimer, *Dialectic of Enlightenment: Philosophical Fragments* (Stanford: Stanford University Press, 2002).

36 This story recalls that of the historian Rolf Wiggershaus, who also discusses the event that revealed the gap between theory and action. With regard to the heckling in question, he wrote that "it was rebellious women members of the SDS [Sozialistische Deutsche Studentenbund] who were responsible. They had formed a Women's Council in 1968, and were among the pioneers of the women's movement." Rolf Wiggershaus, *The Frankfurt School* (Cambridge: Polity, 1994), 635.

37 Letter from Marcuse to Adorno: "We cannot ignore the fact that these students have been influenced by us (and not least by you) . . . And this fresh air is not that of 'left-wing fascism' (*contradicto in adjecto!*), it is the air that we (or at least I) also wanted to breathe one day, and which is certainly not the air of the establishment." Herbert Marcuse quoted by Wiggershaus, *Frankfurt School*, 633–4.

38 Adorno's resistance to Walter Benjamin's ideas about the "human body as a measure of concreteness" is revealed by Angela Cozea, who notes the Adorno–Benjamin correspondence as evidence of their disagreement in this matter. See Angela Cozea, "Habiter en *kosmopolite*: enquête sur les modes de comportement," *Horizons philosophiques* 17 (2) 2007: 75–100.

39 I am referring here to the disputes of 1999 and 2009, which are examined in chapter 4.

40 The first and third chapters of this book have been translated into English: "Mobilization of the Planet from the Spirit of Self-Intensification," transl.

H. Ziegler, *Drama Review*, 50 (4) 2006: 36–43; "Eurotaoism," transl. M. Eldred, in T. Darby, B. Egyed, and B. Jones (eds.), *Nietzsche and the Rhetoric of Nihilism* (Ottawa: Carleton University Press, 1989), 99–116.

41 Ernst Jünger (1895–1998) was a German writer and philosopher who served with distinction in the German army in both world wars. *Storm of Steel* (London: Penguin, 2004), his best-known novel, was first published in 1920.

42 Sloterdijk, "Mobilization of the Planet from the Spirit of Self-Intensification," 36.

43 Sloterdijk, "Mobilization of the Planet from the Spirit of Self-Intensification," 37.

44 Sloterdijk, "Mobilization of the Planet from the Spirit of Self-Intensification," 39.

45 Ernst Jünger, *Der Arbeiter* (Stuttgart: Klett-Cotta, 2014).

46 Sloterdijk, "Mobilization of the Planet from the Spirit of Self-Intensification," 41.

47 Sloterdijk, "Mobilization of the Planet from the Spirit of Self-Intensification," 41.

48 It is also naturally a part of sporting activities. Among thousands of examples, consider "Safe is Death," the mobilizing maxim employed by John Tortorella, former coach of the Tampa Bay Lightning, who led his team to the 2004 National Hockey League championship. The idea that rest leads to death is meant to keep the champion in action.

49 Sloterdijk, "Mobilization of the Planet from the Spirit of Self-Intensification," 39.

50 Sloterdijk, "Mobilization of the Planet from the Spirit of Self-Intensification," 40.

51 In this section devoted to nuclear catastrophes, Sloterdijk inserts as a visual subtext a series of biblical frescos of the Last Judgment.

52 Tuinen, *Peter Sloterdijk*, 42.

53 Heidegger wrote *Being and Time* (Malden: Blackwell, 1962), first published in 1927, in his Todtnauberg cabin in the Black Forest, which has become a destination for philosophical pilgrimages, even for Sloterdijk on his bicycle: "we looked out from outside of Heidegger's cabin, located high on a hill with an expansive view of a sloping flatlands that opens up like the opening scene of the 'clearing'" (ZT 245).

54 At Sloterdijk's request, this title was even abandoned in the French translation and changed for a title à la Jünger: *La mobilisation infinie* [*Infinite Mobilization*], transl. H. Hildenbrand (Paris: Bourgois, 2000), 9.

55 A rewriting of a sentence from the first chapter of the *Tao Te King*: "The Tao that can be spoken is not the eternal Tao."

56 Sloterdijk, "Mobilization of the Planet from the Spirit of Self-Intensification," 42. Chapter 4 will return to this terse declaration in its discussion of Sloterdijk's dispute with representatives of the Frankfurt School in his defense of the honor of productive citizens (*Leistungsträgern*). We will see at this point that the idleness of dropouts and the song of nightingales appear to be less attractive, at least relative to the rhetoric of pride employed by hawks of steel.

57 Sloterdijk, *Zorn und Zeit: Politisch-psychologischer Versuch* (Frankfurt am Main: Suhrkamp, 2006).

58 In a 2013 text, he points to the controversy surrounding his talk "Rules for the Human Zoo" (see chapters 2 and 4) and the September 11, 2001, attacks as two decisive events in the evolution of his thinking (RNU 35–43). With regard to 9/11, he indicates that he became aware of the fact that democracy had enemies, but that it was in no shape to fight (RNU 44).

59 Sloterdijk, *Luftbeben: An den Quellen des Terrors* (Frankfurt am Main: Suhrkamp, 2002).

60 See also Sloterdijk, "Atmospheric Politics," in Latour and Weibel, *Making Things Public*, 944–51.

61 Although Sloterdijk was aware that Fukuyama was a student of Leo Strauss (RT 233n), he said that Strauss and his school "have been unjustly claimed by political neoconservatives in the United States" (RT 23). This formulation of things is amusing and pleads for political recuperation; however, it seeks above all to ignore the fact that Allan Bloom, another of Strauss's students, had access to the White House via his former students who had recycled themselves as Washington apparatchiks. For a caustic portrayal of Bloom, see Saul Bellow's novel *Ravelstein* (New York: Viking, 2000), and for a more serious portrait of the Straussians behind aggressive American policies on the heels of 9/11, see Anne Norton, *Leo Strauss and the Politics of American Empire* (New Haven: Yale University Press, 2004).

62 For these two reasons some critics spoke of a "chatty, mediocre, *furiously* Nietzschean book" (Erik Bordeleau, "Sloterdijk and the Question of Action," in W. Schinkel and L. Noordegraaf-Eelens [eds.], *In Medias Res: Peter Sloterdijk's Spherological Poetics of Being* [Amsterdam: Amsterdam University Press, 2011], 182n); that is, "an ethical drive of an aristocratic nature" (Miguel de Beistegui, "Anger and Time: A Critical Assessment," *Society and Space* 27 [1] 2009: 168–73 at 169), or a "counterrevolutionary agenda," defined as "a rather reactionary stand towards the progressive movements of modernity" (Evgeni V. Pavlov, "Banking on Rage: Sloterdijk's Thymotic Counterrevolution," *Parallax* 17 [2] 2001: 126–30 at 129).

63 The 2010 English translation did not keep this inversion, found in the original German title, unlike the French translation, *Colère et temps: essai politico-psychologique*, transl. O. Mannoni (Paris: Maren Sell, 2007).

64 Plato, *The Republic*, transl. A. Bloom (New York: Basic Books, 1991), 120 [430e].

65 Plato, *Republic*, 119 [440a].

66 In the chapter devoted to communism, Sloterdijk typically talks about "leftist fascism" and, in so doing, bases himself on conservative historians such as Ernst Nolte and François Furet to legitimize this kind of declaration: "Lenin's directives from the late fall of 1917 onward initiated the first authentic fascist initiatives of the twentieth century" (RT 150; see also AP 89). The critique of historical revisionism insists on the militant and viscerally anti-communist nature of declarations of this kind. Losurdo, for instance, describes the object of his critique thus: "The triumph of historical revisionism now produces a compact ideology little concerned with distinctions and which only puts Jacobinism and Bolshevism on trial" (Domenico Losurdo, *Le révisionnisme en histoire* [Paris: Albin Michel, 2006], 25).

67 Costas Douzinas and Slavoj Žižek (eds.), *The Idea of Communism* (London: Verso, 2010).

68 Žižek quoted by Stuart Elden, "Worlds, Engagements, Temparements," in Elden, *Sloterdijk Now*, 2. Žižek briefly discusses the arguments contained in *Rage and Time*, particularly the idea of magnanimity of *thymos*. See Slavoj Žižek, *In Defence of Lost Causes* (London: Verso, 2008), 373–4.

69 Slavoj Žižek, *First as Tragedy, Then as Farce* (London: Verso, 2009), 73. For a critical study of Žižek's provocative and pedagogical apology for violence, see Alexander Del Duca, *Between Marxism and Postmodernism: Slavoj Žižek Doing the Impossible* (University of Ottawa: Thesis, 2009), http://hdl.handle.net/10393/24079

70 "A distinctive mark of Peter Sloterdijk's philosophy, especially within the context of German tradition, seems to be its striking serenity . . . This detached attitude appears to save psychic energy and to subsequently allow for a pleasurable release in beautiful and witty poetic verbalizations." But this love of the object has been transformed into a disappointed language of forgetfulness and decline, as the author "describes our contemporary period as marked by a specific oblivion: *forgetfulness of pride* . . . Here again a certain shift in Sloterdijk's methodical approach becomes visible." Robert Pfaller, "Disinhibition, Subjectivity, and Pride. Or: Guess Who is Looking?" in Schinkel and Noordegraaf-Eelens, *In Medias Res*, 67–8.

71 Herbert Marcuse, *Eros and Civilization* (London: Routledge, 1987). For Marcuse, the flipside of *eros* is not *thymos*, but thanatos (the death drive).

72 Pfaller, "Disinhibition, Subjectivity, and Pride," 77.

73 Pfaller, "Disinhibition, Subjectivity, and Pride," 69.

74 Pfaller, "Disinhibition, Subjectivity, and Pride," 80.

Chapter 2   Anthropotechnics

1 Sigmund Freud, *On Dreams* (New York: Rebman, 1914), 59.

2 Sébastien Mussi, "Préludes à *Sphères*: L'amorce du grand récit fantastique de Peter Sloterdijk. Une lecture de *La domestication de l'Être*," *Horizons philosophiques* 17 (2) 2007: 41–54 at 42.

3 Sloterdijk is mistrustful of the *antihumanist* label that in his view is too often applied to Heidegger's work. He feels that it is a "tortured formulation that suggests something like a metaphysical form of misanthropy" (RHZ 17).

4 Sloterdijk, *Versprechen auf Deutsch: Rede über das eigene Land* (Frankfurt am Main: Suhrkamp, 1990).

5 Sloterdijk, *Im selben Boot: Versuch über die Hyperpolitik* (Frankfurt am Main: Suhrkamp, 1993).

6 Sloterdijk, *Falls Europa Erwacht: Gedanken zum Programm einer Weltmacht am Ende des Zeitalters seiner politischen Absence* (Frankfurt am Main: Suhrkamp, 1994).

7 Sloterdijk, *Der starke Grund zusammen zu sein: Erinnerungen an die Erfindung des Volkes* (Frankfurt am Main: Suhrkamp, 1998).

8 Martin Heidegger, "Letter on Humanism," in Heidegger, *Pathmarks* (Cambridge: Cambridge University Press, 1998), 239–76.

9 Friedrich Nietzsche, *Thus Spoke Zarathustra* (Cambridge: Cambridge University Press, 2006), 133–5.

10 Sloterdijk, "Anthropo-Technology," *New Perspectives Quarterly* 21 (4) 2004: 40–7 at 42–3. This article is the English-language translation of a few passages from the chapter "Domestikation des Seins" in NG.

11 In fact, Sloterdijk borrows from Paul Alsberg (1883–1965), who is viewed as one of the founders of contemporary philosophical anthropology and one of the main influences on Max Scheler, Arnold Gehlen, and Dieter Claessens. Sloterdijk refers to Alsberg's 1922 work *Das Menschheitsrätsel* (*The Enigma of Mankind*, not translated). The use of these nearly 100-year-old references shows that Sloterdijk is not part of current debates; rather, he grapples here and there with the elements of an anthropological fable that, in the case of Alsberg's or Bolk's ideas, were ready to hand for the Heidegger of *Being and Time* (1927).

12 I use here Marie-Ève Morin's English-language translation of this excerpt from her "The Coming-to-the-World of the Human Animal," in Elden, *Sloterdijk Now*, 82.

13 Morin, "The Coming-to-the-World of the Human Animal," 83.

14 Mussi, "Préludes à *Sphères*," 42.

15 "We are now upon the plane where there is mainly technology"; in French in the original. Sloterdijk makes an ironic allusion to Jean-Paul Sartre here: "We are now upon the plane where there are only men."

16 This is the concept of *Körperausschaltung* (literally "shutting down of the body"), borrowed from Alsberg and subsequently rearticulated by Dieter Claessens and Hans Blumenberg (NG 179).

17 Louis Bolk (1866–1930) and his 1926 book *Das Problem der Menschwerdung* (*The Problem of Human Development*, not translated).

18 Thanks to Simon Labrecque, postdoctoral fellow at the University of Ottawa, for this highly ironic and delicious morsel.

19 Sloterdijk, "Anthropo-Technology," 45.

20 As either a symptom of repression or the occlusion of this polemical episode, Sloterdijk no longer mentions the events of 1999 when he talks about "Rules for the Human Zoo." Rather, he refers to his 1997 Basel talk (see MCL 10), which did not attract the same public attention as did his Elmau talk two years later.

21 Sloterdijk's athletic models are all males. This fascination with *Homo erectus* reinforces the idea of a phallic fixation, one that has been criticized by Babette Babich (see chapter 1, n[26]).

22 This is clearly a conservative vocabulary. Although Sloterdijk, like Nietzsche, wants to de-Christianize the vocabulary of exercising, practicing, and elevating, this terrain is already well circumscribed by Catholicism and its athletes. Indeed, it was in these acrobatic words that Pope John Paul II settled the case of Galileo in a speech that neglected to acknowledge the church's wrongful persecution of the "horizontal science" of physics: "It is only this vertical direction which can give full meaning to man's being and action, because it situates him in relation to his origin and his end" (*L'Osservatore Romano*, November, 4, 1992).

23 Friedrich Nietzsche, *On the Genealogy of Morality* (Cambridge: Cambridge University Press, 2007).

24 This was the later Nietzsche who sketched the contours of a general ascetology: "It was only the later Nietzsche, in his dietological reflections of the

1880s – recall the corresponding pages in his self-crucifixion text *Ecce Homo* – who offered points of departure for a doctrine of life practice, or a general ascetology" (MCL 6).

25 Sloterdijk's interest in Foucault dates back to the 1970s. In Sloterdijk's *You Must Change Your Life*, transl. W. Hoban (Cambridge: Polity, 2013), Foucault is among the most cited authors, behind Nietzsche and in front of Heidegger. In this return to his roots, Sloterdijk distances himself from the "middle period" Foucault (MCL 318) who "exaggerated" the weight of repression in the disciplinary process. Sloterdijk prefers the very early and very late Foucault, who was acutely aware of "tragic verticality" and used a corresponding vocabulary: self-concern, self-culture, and struggle with oneself (MCL 149).

26 Foucault, quoted in MCL (159).

27 See Joseph Sieyès, *What is the Third Estate?* (London: Pall Mall Press, 1963).

28 See Jacques Rancière, *The Ignorant Schoolmaster: Five Lessons in Intellectual Emancipation* (Stanford: Stanford University Press, 1991).

29 The difference in treatment of Bourdieu's and Luhmann's sociologies is paradoxical. While critiquing the former here, Sloterdijk praises the latter on several occasions (see MCL 43; NG 82–141; SIII 736–9). He roundly criticizes Bourdieu for overlooking the "authenticity" of those who avoid their class destiny, whereas Luhmann comes down in favor of an even more implacable determinism. Indeed, Luhmann radically suppresses the idea of the individual (and "will," its corollary) to the benefit of the reified existence of social, differentiated, and self-referential subsystems that even more cynically annihilate the possibility of the exceptional hero so hoped for by Sloterdijk. Where Bourdieu theorizes individuals in their relationship to sociality (there is no field that is not filled with individual positions), Luhmann describes the logics that suppress the hypothesis of the individual and of social change. See Niklas Luhmann, *Social Systems* (Stanford: Stanford University Press, 1995).

30 Pierre Bourdieu, *Sketch for Self-Analysis* (Chicago: University of Chicago Press, 2008), 102.

31 Bourdieu, *Sketch for Self-Analysis*, 113.

32 Sloterdijk notes that the "*Great Soviet Encyclopedia* included the term 'anthropotechnics' in its third volume as early as 1926" (MCL 481).

33 Taking up the arguments of historical revisionists such as Ernst Nolte and François Furet, Sloterdijk frees National Socialism from exclusive ownership of death-camp culture with the help of an arithmetic argument: "the world of Nazi camps lasted for just twelve years, those of the Soviet Union almost seventy years" (MCL 427). Of whether or not Nazism was akin to slave-based, racist, and colonialist empires headquartered in Euro-American democracies, nothing is said. For another story, see Domenico Losurdo, *Liberalism: A Counter-History* (New York: Verso, 2014).

Chapter 3   Spherology

1 Don Ihde, "Deromanticizing Heidegger," in Ihde, *Postphenomenology: Essays in the Postmodern Context* (Evanston: Northwestern University Press, 1993),

103. What is meant here is postphenomenology in a slightly different sense than that of Ihde, who is not overly concerned with the anguish and denseness of Heidegger's thought.

2 Heidegger, *Being and Time*, 146.

3 Latour, "Spheres and Networks," 140.

4 Bruno Latour, *Reassembling the Social* (Oxford: Oxford University Press, 2005), 179.

5 At the very least, it is a "rewriting and challenging of the Heideggerian understanding of human existence" (Morin, "The Coming-to-the-World of the Human Animal," 77).

6 Vis-à-vis Heidegger's being-toward-death, Hannah Arendt had opposed praise of natality and the capacity for undertaking something anew: the beginning. Once again, Sloterdijk notes Arendt's gesture as a source of inspiration (ZT 281) for his natal thinking, which he had initially explored during a Frankfurt seminar (see ZWK). See also Sjoerd van Tuinen, "Über philosophischen Selbstgenuss, therapeutische Gelassenheit und natale Differenz," in K. Hemelsoet, M. Jongen, and S. van Tuinen (eds.), *Die Vermessung des Ungeheuren: Philosophie nach Peter Sloterdijk* (Munich: Fink, 2009), 163–72.

7 Sloterdijk has already cut the ground from under the feet of his copyist-readers: "In itself, a quote is a risk for the person who quotes, and things should remain that way" (SIII 866).

8 Nigel Thrift, "Space," *Theory, Culture & Society* 23 (2–3) 2006: 139–46 at 140.

9 Elsewhere this tripartite framework is ironically associated with theology: "Theologians, as you know, arrange their thoughts preferably into three chapters because they like transposing themselves into God's interiority, where the triad sets the tone" (AP 2).

10 Claessens cited by Sloterdijk (SII 205).

11 Sloterdijk, *Falls Europa Erwacht*.

12 "The latest version of the witness myth, produced by Luhmann's system theory, discusses an observer who watches others' action intelligently" (AP 82).

13 Dostoyevsky bases this tale on his visit to London's Crystal Palace, an immense structure opened by Queen Victoria at the 1851 World's Fair.

14 Sloterdijk uses the word *Entlastung*, the literal translation of which could be *discharge*. However, the translator Wieland Hoban prefers to use *relief* in excerpts from WIC.

15 Sloterdijk's *In the World Interior of Capital*, transl. W. Hoban (Cambridge: Polity, 2013), is an outgrowth of the *Spheres* project. Its first part is an enhanced version of ch. 8 of the initial publication of *Globen* (published in English as *Globes: Spheres Volume II*, transl. W. Hoban [Los Angeles: Semiotext(e), 2014]) and its second part resonates with the third chapter of *Schäume* (see SIII 671–859), which also looks at the generalization of luxury and indulgence.

16 Gabriel Tarde, *Monadologie et sociologie* (Paris: Institut Synthélabo, 1999), 56–7.

17 I quote here the English translation by D. Fabricius, published as "Cell Block, Egospheres, Self-Container," *Log* 10, Summer/Fall 2007: 89–108 at 90.

18 Sloterdijk, "Cell Block, Egospheres, Self-Container," 92.

19 This translation is by S. A. Butler, published as "Geometry in the Colossal: The Project of Metaphysical Globalization," *Society and Space* 27 (1) 2009: 29–40 at 32.
20 Sloterdijk, "Geometry in the Colossal," 31.
21 Heidegger quoted by Sloterdijk, "Geometry in the Colossal," 29.
22 Sloterdijk, "Spheres Theory. Talking to Myself About the Poetics of Space," *Harvard Design Magazine* 30 2009: 1–8 at 1–2.
23 Luis Castro Nogueira, "Bubbles, Globes, Wrappings, and *Plektopoi*: Minimal Notes to Rethink Metaphysics from the Standpoint of the Social Sciences," *Society and Space* 27 (1) 2009: 87–104 at 99. The author draws our attention to a few fallacies that accompany Sloterdijk's enthusiasm for grand narratives and, consequently, steer him away from the social sciences: "Like . . . other great critics of metaphysics, Sloterdijk exaggerates, finally, the power of the great philosophical imaginaries as if they were the authentic ontological musculatures that fold the tents, creases, and wrappings of the day-to-day life of millions of individuals in the context of which the same, divine, tragicomedy would have been played out for 2000 years. Something by all accounts, in itself, once again metaphysical" (101).
24 Castro Nogueira, "Bubbles, Globes, Wrappings, and *Plektopoi*," 100.
25 This translation is by Wieland Hoban, published as *Globes*, 135–6.

Chapter 4   Controversy

1 Sloterdijk, "Das elfte Gebot: die progressive Einkommenssteuer," *Frankfurter Allgemeine Zeitung*, September 27, 2009.
2 Published in the June 13, 2009, edition of the *Frankfurter Allgemeine Zeitung*, this text was the source of the ensuing dispute with Honneth and a large part of the German intelligentsia. There is a partial English translation as "The Grasping Hand" (http://www.city-journal.org/2010/20_1_snd -democratic-state.html). Suhrkamp issued a compilation of articles and interviews by Sloterdijk during the few months that this debate lasted (*Die nehmende Hand und die gebende Seite* [Berlin: Suhrkamp, 2010]).
3 While being applauded as a German scholar, Sloterdijk also appeared regularly on national television with his own show, *Das Philosophische Quartett* (until 2012), in addition to numerous other appearances in cultural and public affairs programs. The most prestigious German newspapers and magazines (e.g., *Die Welt*, *Frankfurter Allgemeine Zeitung*, *Süddeutsche Zeitung*, and *Der Spiegel*) constantly solicit Sloterdijk's views on national and international issues.
4 Ulrich J. Schneider, "The Situation of the Philosophy, the Culture of the Philosophers: Philosophy in the New Germany," *Social Research* 64 (2) 1997 : 281–300 at 294.
5 From chancellor Konrad Adenauer's inaugural address in 1949 on Germany's crimes, Karl Jaspers's thoughts about the atomic bomb (*Die Atombombe und die Zukunft des Menschens*, 1956), and Adorno's prescriptions about the duty of memory (*Was bedeutet: Aufarbeitung der Vergangenheit*, 1959) to Willy Brandt's speech on Ostpolitik in 1966, to Rudi Dutschke's leftist warning shots in 1967 and to Helmut Schmidt's defense of the

justification of the antiterrorist state (*Rede in der Antiterror-debatte*, 1975): the first decades of the German Federal Republic were punctuated by these striking debates that affected this democratic regime's domestic and foreign policies alike.

6 Jan-Werner Müller, *Another Country: German Intellectuals, Unification and National Identity* (New Haven: Yale University Press, 2000), 14.

7 From 1982 to 1998, Christian Democrat chancellor Helmut Kohl, who resolutely shepherded through the reforms of German reunification, ruled over federal politics for five consecutive terms. Although this period was certainly less turbulent than earlier decades with their cultural confrontations, it still had its noteworthy debates. In 1986, the historian and student of Heidegger Ernst Nolte initiated a debate over the historical singularity of Nazi crimes (*Vergangenheit, die nicht vergehen will*, 1986). This dispute pitted revisionists, led by Nolte, against left-wing critics, led by Jürgen Habermas, who had absolutely no tolerance for shifts away from the duty of memory and who condemned conservative historians seeking to free Germany from its burden and its historical obligation. Since the enemies of our enemies are often our friends, Sloterdijk takes up Nolte's revisionist thesis on several occasions (see RNU 150 and AP 89).

8 Heinz-Ulrich Nennen, *Philosophie in Echtzeit. Die Sloterdijk-Debatte: Chronik einer Inszenierung* (Würzburg: Königshausen & Neumann, 2003), 74.

9 Nennen, *Philosophie in Echtzeit*, 116.

10 Nennen, *Philosophie in Echtzeit*, 74.

11 Pierre Bourdieu and Loïc Wacquant, *An Invitation to Reflexive Sociology* (Chicago: University of Chicago Press, 1992), 101:"[The] field as a structure of objective relations between positions of force undergirds and guides the strategies whereby the occupants of these positions seek, individually or collectively, to safeguard or improve their position and to impose the principle of hierarchization most favorable to their own products. The strategies of agents depend on their position in the field, that is, in the distribution of the specific capital, and on the perception that they have of the field depending on the point of view they take on the field as a view taken from a point in the field."

12 Meggle quoted by Nennen, *Philosophie in Echtzeit*, 61. Meggle was in attendance for the exchange between Sloterdijk and Friedländer, during which Friedländer suddenly left for a telephone interview with an Israeli media outlet set up long ahead of time. This rapid exit was enough to provide Meggle with the ingredients of an apparent malaise, despite the fact that the two interested parties denied this interpretation of things.

13 Published on October 24, 1999, by express order of Suhrkamp's president Siegfried Unseld, the transcript of Sloterdijk's talk was leaked a few times to the media by mid-September and was downloaded 60,000 times during the same period.

14 Max Pensky, *The Ends of Solidarity* (Albany: State University of New York Press, 2008), 214.

15 Thomas Assheuer, "Das Zarathustra-Projekt: Der Philosoph Peter Sloterdijk fordert eine gentechnische Revision der Menscheit," *Die Zeit*, September 2, 1999.

16 Reinhard Mohr, "Züchter des Übermenschen," *Der Spiegel*, September 6, 1999.

17 Mohr, "Züchter des Übermenschen." Internationally renowned author Peter Handke provoked a heated debate in 1996 when he described Serbia as one of the victims of the Balkan war. In 2006, he continued to provoke media sensitivities with his heartfelt panegyric given on the occasion of Slobodan Milošević's funeral. Because of this speech, he was denied the Heinrich Heine Award, which the city of Düsseldorf was getting ready to give him.

18 Nennen, *Philosophie in Echtzeit*, 231.

19 Sloterdijk, "Die Kritische Theorie ist tot," *Die Zeit*, September 9, 1999.

20 Jürgen Habermas, "Post vom bösen Geist," *Die Zeit*, September 16, 1999.

21 Nennen, Philosophie in Echtzeit, 182.

22 This fax sent by Habermas from the city of Starnberg is, along with 9/11, one of the two most traumatic events that Sloterdijk comes back to in *Reflexionen eines nicht mehr Unpolitischen* [*Reflections of a Not Anymore Unpolitical*] (RNU 37).

23 I discuss this generational transmission of the polemic in Jean-Pierre Couture, "A Public Intellectual," in Elden, *Sloterdijk Now*, 99–104.

24 Axel Honneth, "Fataler Tiefsinn aus Karlsruhe," *Die Zeit*, September 24, 2009.

25 Sloterdijk, "Die Revolution der gebenden Hand," in F. Schirrmacher and T. Strobl (eds.), *Die Zukunft des Kapitalismus* (Berlin: Suhrkamp, 2010), 60–70 at 69–70. Originally published in *Frankfurter Allgemeine Zeitung*, June 13, 2009.

26 Sloterdijk refers to these productive citizens with the term *Leistungsträgern*, which literally means "those who carry the weight of performance" and which connotes an athletic vocabulary (top performers, key players, go-to-people, achievers, doers, etc.).

27 It is Rousseau whom Sloterdijk initially names as being the source of this hatred of property. In his diary, he even goes so far as to describe Rousseau as the quintessence of a thankless individual: "too proud to be a man who takes, the parvenu author wants to appear as a man who, in all truth, gives" (ZT 279).

28 Sloterdijk, "Die Revolution der gebenden Hand," 70.

29 Honneth, "Fataler Tiefsinn aus Karlsruhe."

30 Sloterdijk, "Wider der Verteufelung der Leistungsträger," *Süddeutsche Zeitung*, January 5, 2010.

31 Sloterdijk, "Wider der Verteufelung der Leistungsträger."

32 Paul Kirchhof, "Die Steuer ist ein Preis der Freiheit," *Frankfurter Allgemeine Zeitung*, November 7, 2009.

33 Ulrich Beck, "Schlemmen für die Dritte Welt," *Cicero*, December 2009.

34 See Jan Rehmann and Thomas Wagner (eds.), *Angriff der Leistungträger? Das Buch zur Sloterdijk-Debatte* (Hamburg: Argument, 2010).

35 Honneth, "Fataler Tiefsinn aus Karlsruhe."

36 Sloterdijk, "Das elfte Gebot."

37 Axel Honneth, "Nach neuen Formen suchen," *Kölner Stadt-Anzeiger*, December 16, 2009.

38 Sloterdijk, "Aufbruch der Leistungsträger," *Cicero*, November 2009.

39 Sloterdijk, "Wider der Verteufelung der Leistungsträger."
40 It is in these terms that Novalis describes the Romantic art of writing: "The art of writing books is still to be discovered. But it is on the verge of being discovered. Fragments of this kind are like a literary sowing of the fields. Of course, there may be many sterile seeds in them. Nevertheless, if only a few of them blossom!" Novalis, "Pollen," in F. C. Beiser (ed.), *The Early Political Writings of the German Romantics* (Cambridge: Cambridge University Press, 1996), 9–31 at 31.
41 Sloterdijk, who prefers provocation to intersubjective calm, wryly admits to the epithets applied to him during the income tax scandal: "In light of everything that we hear, the dark side of my imago is an arrogant hybrid of Dieter Bohlen, Muammar Khadafy and Carl Schmitt" (ZT 325), and then concludes: "How does one resist public attacks? Remember the state you were in before you read in the newspaper that you were a swine" (ZT 347).
42 The Stoic Cicero (106–43 BC) disagreed with the Epicurean image of the inactive, blessed gods. To Rome's bohemian youth, he wrote: " '[Gods] have nothing to do' your teacher says. Epicurus truly, like indolent boys, thinks nothing is preferable to idleness." Cicero, *On the Nature of the Gods* (London: H. G. Bohn, 1853), 36.
43 Sloterdijk, "Die Eingeweide des Zeitgeistes," *Der Spiegel*, October 26, 2009.
44 Respectively, prime minister of the United Kingdom from 1997 to 2007 (Labour Party), prime minister of France from 1997 to 2002 (Socialist Party), and chancellor of Germany from 1998 to 2005 (Social Democratic Party).
45 In 2001, Schröder made his position about the falseness of a right to be lazy clear: "those who can work, but do not want to, cannot rely on solidarity. There is no right to laziness in our society!" (*Der Spiegel*, April 6, 2001). The chancellor also approved of the affirmation of uninhibited pride in being German: "I am proud of the achievements of people and of democratic culture. In this sense, I am a German patriot who is proud of his country" (*Süddeutsche Zeitung*, March 20, 2001). Since achievements and pride are keywords of social democracy in power, it is unlikely that there would be a real gap between Sloterdijk's political and philosophical preferences.
46 Sloterdijk, "Wider der Verteufelung der Leistungsträger." He had already expressed his Americanophilia in an October 20, 2009, journal entry: "They begin with the idea that they are there to help themselves and to help others for as long and as often as necessary" (ZT 304).
47 Sloterdijk, *Die nehmende Hand und die gebende Seite*, 31.
48 Plato was an advisor to the tyrant Dion of Syracuse in Sicily. However, the relationship turned sour.
49 Sloterdijk, "Aufbruch der Leistungsträger".
50 Sjoerd van Tuinen, "A Thymotic Left? Peter Sloterdijk and the Psychopolitics of Ressentiment," *Symploke* 18 (2) 2010 : 47–64.
51 Sjoerd van Tuinen, "From Psychopolitics to Cosmopolitics: The Problem of Ressentiment," in Elden, *Sloterdijk Now*, 37–57 at 54. With a few nuances and a hint of hesitation, Tuinen wonders at the end of his article whether

this distance relative to a kynical enlightenment of gay science might not be a "circumstantial departure from the rest of his work" (57).

52 "When I heard of the fires in Paris, I felt for several days annihilated and was overwhelmed by fears and doubt; the entire scholarly, scientific, philosophical, and artistic existence seemed an absurdity, if a single day could wipe out the most glorious work of art, even whole periods of art; I clung with the earnest conviction to the metaphysical value of art, which cannot exist for the sake of poor human beings but which has higher missions to fulfill. But even when the pain was at its worst, I could not cast a stone against those blasphemers, who were to me only carriers of the general guilt, which gives much food for thought." Nietzsche's letter to Gersdorff, June 21, 1871, in *Selected Letters of Friedrich Nietzsche* (Chicago: Chicago University Press, 1969), 81.

53 Domenico Losurdo, *Nietzsche: Philosophe réactionnaire* (Paris: Delga, 2007), 112.

54 Losurdo, *Nietzsche: Philosophe réactionnaire*, 55.

Chapter 5   Therapy

1 Levi, *Philosophy as Social Expression*, 166–8.

2 Randall Collins, *The Sociology of Philosophies: A Global Theory of Intellectual Change* (Cambridge MA: Harvard University Press, 1998), 636.

3 Sloterdijk is not only a novelist (*Der Zauberbaum* [Frankfurt am Main: Suhrkamp, 1985]) but also the author of the libretto used in Jörg Widmann's 2012 opera *Babylon*. Sloterdijk's ideas about aesthetics are laid out in *The Aesthetic Imperative*, an anthology of short texts and interviews. See *Der ästhetische Imperative* (Hamburg: Philo & Philo Fine Arts, 2007; republished Berlin: Suhrkamp, 2014).

4 Peter Weibel, "Nachwort," in Sloterdijk, *Der ästhetische Imperative*, 491–506 at 506.

5 This mystical avatar of physical science did not outlast its generation, just as alchemy and astrology no longer came to be confused with chemistry and astronomy in the nineteenth century. "*Naturphilosophie* . . . sought to integrate scientific ideas with mystical ideas about the unity of the world (e.g., the idea of a world soul, *Weltseele*)." René ten Bos, "Towards an Amphibious Anthropology: Water and Peter Sloterdijk," *Society and Space* 27 (1) 2009: 73–86 at 75.

6 Friedrich Schlegel, "Ideas," in Beiser, *Early Writings of the German Romantics*, 125–40 at 134.

7 Safranski, *Romantik: Eine deutsche Affäre*, 178–9.

8 Keith Ansell-Pearson, "The Transfiguration of Existence and Sovereign Life: Sloterdijk and Nietzsche on Posthuman and Superhuman Futures," *Society and Space* 27 (1) 2009: 139–56 at 144.

9 I use Efraín Kristal's English-language translation of this excerpt from his "Literature in Sloterdijk's Philosophy," in Elden, *Sloterdijk Now*, 147–64 at 149.

10 Frederick C. Beiser, "Introduction," in Besier, *Early Writings of the German Romantics*, xvii.

11 "In the Romantic scheme of things, from Friedrich Schlegel to Nietzsche, the Dionysian energy at work in art is not directed towards a radiant hereafter but towards the half-light of the prodigious and dynamic vital process" (Safranski, *Romantik: Eine deutsche Affäre*, 288).

12 In line with Heine, who, with the public of his time in mind, provided a critical summary of German thought via the personalities of its most illustrious figures, Sloterdijk never separates an author's life from his or her work. See Sloterdijk, *Philosophical Temperaments: From Plato to Foucault*, transl. C. Davis (New York: Columbia University Press, 2013).

13 Mikhail Bakhtin, *Rabelais and His World* (Bloomington: Indiana University Press, 1993), 19.

14 Bakhtin, *Rabelais and His World*, 21.

15 Ansell-Pearson, "Transfiguration of Existence and Sovereign Life," 145.

16 Henk Oosterling, "Interest and Excess of Modern Man's Radical Mediocrity: Rescaling Sloterdijk's Grandiose Aesthetic Strategy," *Cultural Politics* 3 (3) 2007: 357–80 at 360–1.

17 Although spherology (1998–2004) insists on the "We" to weaken the fiction of the "I," later anthropotechnics (2009) opts instead for the heroism and the will of the "I" as a means of getting out from under the weight of habit and repetition. Even though these approaches could be viewed as distinct and even if a creative interpretation could make them compatible, this gap is symptomatic of a stimulating problem in Sloterdijk's recent thought, examined in chapter 2.

18 Here again, argues Sloterdijk, it is appropriate to read the *single* phenomenon through a dyadic lens: "The condition for initiating self-coupling is the media that we have designated by the term *egotechniques* – they are common medial vectors of self-complementation and which enable their users constant feedback with themselves and thereby the constitution of a couple with oneself as a surprise internal partner" (SIII 584). Later, Sloterdijk comes back to a dyadic description imbued with the irony of autosexuality: "Apartment onanism, likely anticipated in monastery cells, introduces the complete triangle relationship among the subject, the genitalia and fantasy – from which it follows that masturbatory sexuality certainly introduces a pragmatic abbreviation of the process, though not a structural simplification of the bi-genital act" (SIII 600).

19 Quoted by Sloterdijk from Bruno's *De vinculis in genere* [*A General Account of Bonding*].

20 Quoted by Sloterdijk from Karl Christian Wolfart's *Mesmerismus oder System der Wechselwirkungen* [*Mesmerism, or, System of Interdependencies*].

21 Schlegel, "Ideas," 136.

22 Quoted by Sloterdijk from Nietzsche's letter to Malvida von Meysenburg, April 20, 1883.

23 I would like to thank Jonah Clifford for this apposite remark about Sloterdijk's complete opposition to Freud with regard to viewing language and religion as suspect.

24 Sloterdijk, *Im Schatten des Sinai* (Berlin: Suhrkamp, 2013), 44.

25 Sloterdijk, *Im Schatten des Sinai*, 63.

26 Sloterdijk, *Im Schatten des Sinai*, 61.

Conclusion

1 Sloterdijk, *Philosophical Temperaments*, xix.
2 Robert K. Merton and Elinor Barber, *The Travels and Adventures of Serendipity: A Study in Sociological Semantics* (Princeton: Princeton University Press, 2004), 3.
3 See Dahlia Namian and Carolyne Grimard, "Pourquoi parle-t-on de séren-pidité aujourd'hui?" *SociologieS* 2013, http://sociologies.revues.org/4490

References

Primary Sources

"Anthropo-Technology." *New Perspectives Quarterly* 21 (4) 2004: 40–7.

The Art of Philosophy, transl. K. Margolis. New York: Columbia University Press, 2012.

Der ästhetische Imperative. Hamburg: Philo & Philo Fine Arts, 2007; republished Berlin: Suhrkamp, 2014.

"Atmospheric Politics," in Latour, B. and Weibel, P. (eds.). *Making Things Public: Atmospheres of Democracy*. Cambridge MA: MIT Press, 2005, 944–51.

"Aufbruch der Leistungsträger." *Cicero*, November 2009.

Les battements du monde, with Alain Finkielkraut. Paris: Pauvert, 2003.

Bubbles: Spheres Volume I, transl. W. Hoban. Los Angeles: Semiotext(e), 2011.

"Cell Block, Egospheres, Self-Container," transl. D. Fabricius. *Log* 10, Summer/Fall 2007: 89–108.

Colère et temps: essai politico-psychologique, transl. O. Mannoni. Paris: Maren Sell, 2007.

Critique of Cynical Reason, transl. M. Eldred. Minneapolis: University of Minnesota Press, 1987.

Derrida, An Egyptian, transl. W. Hoban. Cambridge: Polity, 2009.

"Die Eingeweide des Zeitgeistes." *Der Spiegel*, October 26, 2009.

"Das elfte Gebot: die progressive Einkommenssteuer." *Frankfurter Allgemeine Zeitung*, September 27, 2009.

"Eurotaoism," transl. M. Eldred, in Darby, T., Egyed, B., and Jones, B. (eds.). *Nietzsche and the Rhetoric of Nihilism*. Ottawa: Carleton University Press, 1989, 99–116.

Falls Europa Erwacht: Gedanken zum Programm einer Weltmacht am Ende des Zeitalters seiner politischen Absence. Frankfurt am Main: Suhrkamp, 1994.

"Geometry in the Colossal: The Project of Metaphysical Globalization," transl. S. A. Butler. *Society and Space* 27 (1) 2009: 29–40.

Globes: Spheres Volume II, transl. W. Hoban. Los Angeles: Semiotext(e), 2014.

God's Zeal: The Battle of the Three Monotheisms, transl. W. Hoban. Cambridge: Polity, 2009.

"The Grasping Hand." http://www.city-journal.org/2010/20_1_snd-democratic-state.html

Kopernikanische Mobilmachung und ptolemäische Abrüstung. Frankfurt am Main: Suhrkamp, 1986.

"Die Kritische Theorie ist tot." *Die Zeit*, September 9, 1999.

Literatur und Organisation von Lebenserfahrung: Autobiographie der zwanziger Jahre. Munich: Hanser, 1978.

Luftbeben: An den Quellen des Terrors. Frankfurt am Main: Suhrkamp, 2002.

Mein Frankreich. Berlin: Suhrkamp, 2013.

La mobilisation infinie, transl. H. Hildenbrand. Paris: Bourgois, 2000.

"Mobilization of the Planet from the Spirit of Self-Intensification," transl. H. Ziegler. *Drama Review* 50 (4) 2006: 36–43.

Die nehmende Hand und die gebende Seite. Berlin: Suhrkamp, 2010.

Neither Sun nor Death, with Hans-Jürgen Heinrichs, transl. S. Corcoran. Los Angeles: Semiotext(e), 2011.

Nicht gerettet: Versuche nach Heidegger. Frankfurt am Main: Suhrkamp, 2000.

Nietzsche Apostle, transl. S. Corcoran, Los Angeles: Semiotext(e), 2013.

Philosophical Temperaments: From Plato to Foucault, transl. C. Davis. New York: Columbia University Press, 2013.

"Postface à l'édition française de *Règles pour le parc humain*." Paris: Mille et une nuits, 1999.

Rage and Time: A Psychopolitical Investigation, transl. M. Wenning. New York: Columbia University Press, 2010.

Reflexionen eines nicht mehr Unpolitischen. Berlin: Suhrkamp, 2013.

"Die Revolution der gebenden Hand," in Schirrmacher, F. and Strobl, T. (eds.). *Die Zukunft des Kapitalismus*. Berlin: Suhrkamp, 2010, 60–70. Originally published in *Frankfurter Allgemeine Zeitung*, June 13, 2009.

"Rules for the Human Zoo," transl. M. V. Rorty. *Society and Space* 27 (1) 2009: 12–28.

Im Schatten des Sinai (Berlin: Suhrkamp, 2013)

Im selben Boot: Versuch über die Hyperpolitik. Frankfurt am Main: Suhrkamp, 1993.

Selbstversuch: Ein Gespräch mit Carlos Oliveira. Munich: Hanser, 1996.

Sphären II: Globen. Frankfurt am Main: Suhrkamp, 1999.

Sphären III: Schäume. Frankfurt am Main: Suhrkamp, 2004.

"Spheres Theory: Talking to Myself About the Poetics of Space." *Harvard Design Magazine* 30 2009: 1–8.

Der starke Grund zusammen zu sein: Erinnerungen an die Erfindung des Volkes. Frankfurt am Main: Suhrkamp, 1998.

Terror from the Air, transl. S. Corcoran. Los Angeles: Semiotext(e), 2009.

Theory of the Post-War Periods, transl. R. Payne. Vienna: Springer, 2009.

Thinker on Stage: Nietzsche's Materialism, transl. J. O. Daniel. Minneapolis: University of Minnesota Press, 1989.

Die Verachtung der Massen: Versuch über Kulturkämpfe in der modernen Gesellschaft. Frankfurt am Main: Suhrkamp, 2000.

Versprechen auf Deutsch: Rede über das eigene Land. Frankfurt am Main: Suhrkamp, 1990.

"Weimar et la Californie: note sur la crise de la philosophie de l'histoire et sur la prolifération des doctrines holistiques." *Critique* 464–5 1986: 114–27.

Weltfremdheit. Frankfurt am Main: Suhrkamp, 1993.

Zur Welt kommen – Zur Sprache kommen. Frankfurt am Main: Suhrkamp, 1988.

"What Happened in the Twentieth Century? En Route to a Critique of Extremist Reason," *Cultural Politics* 3 (3) 2007: 327–56.

"Wider der Verteufelung der Leistungsträger." *Süddeutsche Zeitung*, January 5, 2010.

In the World Interior of Capital, transl. W. Hoban. Cambridge: Polity, 2013.

You Must Change Your Life, transl. W. Hoban. Cambridge: Polity, 2013.

Der Zauberbaum. Frankfurt am Main: Suhrkamp, 1985.

Zeilen und Tage. Berlin: Suhrkamp, 2012.

Zorn und Zeit: Politisch-psychologischer Versuch. Frankfurt am Main: Suhrkamp, 2006.

Secondary Sources

Ansell-Pearson, Keith. "The Transfiguration of Existence and Sovereign Life: Sloterdijk and Nietzsche on Posthuman and Superhuman Futures." *Society and Space* 27 (1) 2009: 139–56.

Assheuer, Thomas. "Das Zarathustra-Projekt: Der Philosoph Peter Sloterdijk fordert eine gentechnische Revision der Menscheit." *Die Zeit*, September 2, 1999.

Babich, Babette. "Sloterdijk's Cynicism: Diogenes in the Marketplace," in Elden, S. (ed.). *Sloterdijk Now.* Cambridge: Polity, 2012, 17–36.

Beistegui, Miguel de. "Anger and Time: A Critical Assessment." *Society and Space* 27 (1) 2009: 168–73.

Bordeleau, Erik. "Sloterdijk and the Question of Action," in Schinkel, W. and Noordegraaf-Eelens, L. (eds.). *In Medias Res: Peter Sloterdijk's Spherological Poetics of Being*. Amsterdam: Amsterdam University Press, 2011, 165–84.

Bos, René ten. "Towards an Amphibious Anthropology: Water and Peter Sloterdijk." *Society and Space* 27 (1) 2009: 73–86.

Castro Nogueira, Luis. "Bubbles, Globes, Wrappings, and *Plektopoi*: Minimal Notes to Rethink Metaphysics from the Standpoint of the Social Sciences." *Society and Space* 27 (1) 2009: 87–104.

Couture, Jean-Pierre. "A Public Intellectual," in Elden, S. (ed.). *Sloterdijk Now*. Cambridge: Polity, 2012, 99–104.

Cozea, Angela. "Habiter en *kosmopolite*: enquête sur les modes de comportement." *Horizons philosophiques* 17 (2) 2007: 75–100.

Elden, Stuart (ed.). *Sloterdijk Now*. Cambridge: Polity, 2012.

Elden, Stuart. "Worlds, Engagements, Temperaments," in Elden, S. (ed.). *Sloterdijk Now*. Cambridge: Polity, 2012, 1–16.

Elden, Stuart, Mendieta, Eduardo, and Thrift, Nigel (eds.). "Special Issue: The Worlds of Peter Sloterdijk." *Society and Space* 27 (1) 2009.

Giroux, Dalie. "Nietzsche et Sloterdijk, corps en resonance." *Horizons philosophiques* 17 (2) 2007: 101–22.

Habermas, Jürgen. "Post vom bösen Geist." *Die Zeit*, September 16, 1999.

Heinrichs, Hans-Jürgen. *Peter Sloterdijk: Die Kunst des Philosophierens*. Munich: Hanser, 2011.

Honneth, Axel. "Fataler Tiefsinn aus Karlsruhe." *Die Zeit*, September 24, 2009.

Honneth, Axel. "Nach neuen Formen suchen." *Kölner Stadt-Anzeiger*, December 16, 2009.

Kirchhof, Paul. "Die Steuer ist ein Preis der Freiheit." *Frankfurter Allgemeine Zeitung*, November 7, 2009.

Kristal, Efraín. "Literature in Sloterdijk's Philosophy," in Elden, S. (ed.). *Sloterdijk Now*. Cambridge: Polity, 2012, 147–64.

Latour, Bruno. "Spheres and Networks: Two Ways to Reinterpret Globalization." *Harvard Design Magazine* 30 2009: 138–44.

Mohr, Reinhard. "Züchter des Übermenschen." *Der Spiegel*, September 6, 1999.

Morin, Marie-Ève. "The Coming-to-the-World of the Human Animal," in Elden, S. (ed.). *Sloterdijk Now*. Cambridge: Polity, 2012, 77–95.

Mussi, Sébastien. "Préludes à *Sphères*: L'amorce du grand récit fantastique de Peter Sloterdijk. Une lecture de *La domestication de l'Être*." *Horizons philosophiques* 17 (2) 2007: 41–54.

Nennen, Heinz-Ulrich. *Philosophie in Echtzeit Die Sloterdijk-Debatte: Chronik einer Inszenierung*. Würzburg: Königshausen & Neumann, 2003.

Oosterling, Henk. "Interest and Excess of Modern Man's Radical Medi-ocrity: Rescaling Sloterdijk's Grandiose Aesthetic Strategy." *Cultural Politics* 3 (3) 2007: 357–80.

Pavlov, Evgeni V. "Banking on Rage: Sloterdijk's Thymotic Counter-revolution." *Parallax* 17 (2) 2001: 126–30.

Pfaller, Robert. "Disinhibition, Subjectivity, and Pride. Or: Guess Who is Looking?," in Schinkel, W. and Noordegraaf-Eelens, L. (eds.). *In Medias Res: Peter Sloterdijk's Spherological Poetics of Being.* Amsterdam: Amsterdam University Press, 2011, 67–82.

Rehmann, Jan and Wagner, Thomas (eds.). *Angriff der Leistungträger? Das Buch zur Sloterdijk-Debatte.* Hamburg: Argument, 2010.

Safranski, Rüdiger. "Peter Sloterdijk: Meister der fröhlich en Wissen-schaft." *Die Welt*, June 26, 2007.

Schinkel, Willem and Noordegraaf-Eelens, Liesbeth (eds.). *In Medias Res: Peter Sloterdijk's Spherological Poetics of Being.* Amsterdam: Amster-dam University Press, 2011

Tuinen, Sjoerd van. *Peter Sloterdijk: Ein Profil.* Paderborn: Fink, 2007.

Tuinen, Sjoerd van (ed.). "Special Issue on Peter Sloterdijk." *Cultural Politics* 3 (3) 2007.

Tuinen, Sjoerd van. "Über philosophischen Selbstgenuss, thera-peutische Gelassenheit und natale Differenz," in Hemelsoet, K., Jongen, M., and Tuinen, S. van (eds.). *Die Vermessung des Ungeheuren: Philosophie nach Peter Sloterdijk.* Munich: Fink, 2009, 163–72.

Tuinen, Sjoerd van. "A Thymotic Left? Peter Sloterdijk and the Psycho-politics of Ressentiment." *Symploke* 18 (2) 2010: 47–64.

Tuinen, Sjoerd van. "From Psychopolitics to Cosmopolitics: The Problem of Ressentiment," in Elden, S. (ed.). *Sloterdijk Now.* Cam-bridge: Polity, 2012, 37–57.

Weibel, Peter. "Nachwort," in Sloterdijk, P. *Der ästhetische Imperative.* Hamburg: Philo & Philo Fine Arts, 2007, 491–506.

Other Works Cited

Adorno, Theodor and Horkheimer, Max. *Dialectic of Enlightenment: Philosophical Fragments.* Stanford: Stanford University Press, 2002.

Bakhtin, Mikhail. *Rabelais and His World.* Bloomington: Indiana Univer-sity Press, 1993.

Beck, Ulrich. "Schlemmen für die Dritte Welt." *Cicero*, December 2009.

Beiser, Frederick C. (ed.). *The Early Political Writings of the German Romantics.* Cambridge: Cambridge University Press, 1996.

Bellow, Saul. *Ravelstein.* New York: Viking, 2000.

Bourdieu, Pierre. *Sketch for Self-Analysis.* Chicago: University of Chicago Press, 2008.

Bourdieu, Pierre and Wacquant, Loïc. *An Invitation to Reflexive Sociology*. Chicago: University of Chicago Press, 1992.

Cicero. *On the Nature of the Gods*. London: H. G. Bohn, 1853.

Collins, Randall. *The Sociology of Philosophies: A Global Theory of Intellectual Change*. Cambridge MA: Harvard University Press, 1998.

Del Duca, Alexander. *Between Marxism and Postmodernism: Slavoj Žižek Doing the Impossible*. University of Ottawa: Thesis, 2009. http://hdl.handle.net/10393/24079

Douzinas, Costas and Žižek, Slavoj (eds.). *The Idea of Communism*. London: Verso, 2010.

Faye, Jean-Pierre. *L'État total selon Carl Schmitt: ou comment la narration engendre des monstres*. Paris: Germina, 2013.

Foucault, Michel. *The Courage of Truth: The Government of Self and Others II. Lectures at the Collège de France 1983–1984*. New York: Palgrave Macmillan, 2011.

Freud, Sigmund. *On Dreams*. New York: Rebman, 1914.

Freud, Sigmund. *Civilization and Its Discontents*. London: Penguin, 2002.

Groys, Boris and Weibel, Peter (eds.). *Medium Religion: Faith. Religion. Art*. Cologne: König, 2011.

Heidegger, Martin. *Being and Time*. Malden: Blackwell, 1962.

Heidegger, Martin. "Letter on Humanism," in Heidegger, M. *Pathmarks*. Cambridge: Cambridge University Press, 1998, 239–76.

Heine, Heinrich. *Histoire de la religion et de la philosophie en Allemagne*. Paris: Imprimerie nationale, 1993.

Heine, Heinrich. *The Harz Journey and Selected Prose*. London: Penguin, 2006.

Horkheimer, Max. *Between Philosophy and Social Science*. Cambridge MA: MIT Press, 1993.

Ihde, Don. *Postphenomenology: Essays in the Postmodern Context*. Evanston: Northwestern University Press, 1993.

Jünger, Ernst. *Storm of Steel*. London: Penguin, 2004.

Jünger, Ernst. *Der Arbeiter*. Stuttgart: Klett-Cotta, 2014.

Kant, Immanuel. *Practical Philosophy*. Cambridge: Cambridge University Press, 1996.

Kershaw, Ian. *The Nazi Dictatorship: Problems and Perspectives of Interpretation*. London: Arnold Press, 2000.

Latour, Bruno. *Reassembling the Social*. Oxford: Oxford University Press, 2005.

Latour, Bruno and Weibel, Peter (eds.). *Making Things Public: Atmospheres of Democracy*. Cambridge MA: MIT Press, 2005.

Latour, Bruno, Weibel, Peter, and Bigg, Charlotte (eds.). *Iconoclash: Beyond the Image Wars in Science, Religion, and Art*. Cambridge MA: MIT Press, 2002.

Levi, Albert William. *Philosophy as Social Expression*. Chicago: University of Chicago Press, 1974.

Losurdo, Domenico. *Le révisionnisme en histoire*. Paris: Albin Michel, 2006.

Losurdo, Domenico. *Nietzsche: philosophe réactionnaire*. Paris: Delga, 2007.

Losurdo, Domenico. *Liberalism: A Counter-History*. New York: Verso, 2014.

Luhmann, Niklas. *Social Systems*. Stanford: Stanford University Press, 1995.

Lyotard, Jean-François. *The Postmodern Condition: A Report on Knowledge*. Minneapolis: University of Minnesota Press, 1984.

Marcuse, Herbert. *Eros and Civilization*. London: Routledge, 1987.

Merton, Robert K. and Barber, Elinor. *The Travels and Adventures of Serendipity: A Study in Sociological Semantics*. Princeton: Princeton University Press, 2004.

Müller, Jan-Werner. *Another Country: German Intellectuals, Unification and National Identity*. New Haven: Yale University Press, 2000.

Namian, Dahlia and Grimard, Carolyne. "Pourquoi parle-t-on de sérenpidité aujourd'hui?" *SociologieS*, 2013. http://sociologies. revues.org/4490

Niehues-Pröbsting, Heinrich. *Der Kynismus der Diogenes und der Begriff des Zynismus*. Munich: Wilhelm Fink, 1979.

Nietzsche, Friedrich. *Selected Letters of Friedrich Nietzsche*. Chicago: Chicago University Press, 1969.

Nietzsche, Friedrich. *Untimely Meditations*. Cambridge: Cambridge University Press, 1997.

Nietzsche, Friedrich. *Thus Spoke Zarathustra*. Cambridge: Cambridge University Press, 2006.

Nietzsche, Friedrich. *Ecce homo*. Oxford: Oxford University Press, 2007.

Nietzsche, Friedrich. *On the Genealogy of Morality*. Cambridge: Cambridge University Press, 2007.

Norton, Anne. *Leo Strauss and the Politics of American Empire*. New Haven: Yale University Press, 2004.

Novalis. "Pollen," in Beiser, F. C. (ed.). *The Early Political Writings of the German Romantics*. Cambridge: Cambridge University Press, 1996, 9–31.

Pensky, Max. *The Ends of Solidarity*. Albany: State University of New York Press, 2008.

Pinto, Louis. *Les neveux de Zarathoustra*. Paris: Seuil, 1995.

Plato. *The Republic*, transl. A. Bloom. New York: Basic Books, 1991.

Pope John Paul II. *L'Osservatore Romano*, November 4, 1992.

Puységur, Marquis de. *Mémoires pour servir à l'histoire et à l'établissement du magnétisme animal*. Paris: L'Harmattan, 2008.

Rancière, Jacques. *The Ignorant Schoolmaster: Five Lessons in Intellectual Emancipation*. Stanford: Stanford University Press, 1991.

Safranski, Rüdiger. *Romantik: Eine deutsche Affäre*. Munich: Hanser, 2007.

Schlegel, Friedrich. "Ideas," in Beiser, F. C. (ed.). *The Early Political Writings of the German Romantics*. Cambridge: Cambridge University Press, 1996, 125–40.

Schmitt, Carl. *Political Theology: Four Chapters on the Concept of Sovereignty*. Chicago: University of Chicago Press, 2004.

Schneider, Ulrich J. "The Situation of the Philosophy, the Culture of the Philosophers: Philosophy in the New Germany." *Social Research* 64 (2) 1997: 281–300.

Sieyès, Joseph. *What is the Third Estate?* London: Pall Mall Press, 1963.

Spanos, William V. *Heidegger and Criticism: Retrieving the Cultural Politics of Destruction*. Minneapolis: University of Minnesota Press, 1993.

Tarde, Gabriel. *Monadologie et sociologie*. Paris: Institut Synthélabo, 1999.

Thrift, Nigel. "Space." *Theory, Culture & Society* 23 (2–3) 2006: 139–46.

Wiggershaus, Rolf. *The Frankfurt School*. Cambridge: Polity, 1994.

Žižek, Slavoj. *In Defence of Lost Causes*. London: Verso, 2008.

Žižek, Slavoj. *First as Tragedy, Then as Farce*. London: Verso, 2009.

Index